Bears

Bears

Matthias Breiter

Firefly Books

A FIREFLY BOOK

Published by Firefly Books Ltd. 2005

First printing

Publisher Cataloging-in-Publication Data (U.S.)

Breiter, Matthias.
    Bears: a year in the life / Matthias Breiter.
[176] p. : col. photos. ; cm.
Includes bibliographical references and index.
Summary: A year in the life of three bears found in North America: the brown bear, the black bear and the polar bear, Including an examination of hibernation, mating, hunting and feeding.
ISBN 1-55407-077-5
1. Bears. I. Title.
599.78 22   QL737.C27B74 2005

Library and Archives Canada Cataloguing in Publication

Breiter, Matthias
        Bears : a year in the life / Matthias Breiter.
Includes bibliographical references and index.
ISBN 1-55407-077-5
        1. Bears—North America. I. Title.
QL737.C27B73 2005   599.78'097   C2005-901184-X

Published in the United States by
Firefly Books (U.S.) Inc.
P.O. Box 1338, Ellicott Station
Buffalo, New York 14205

Published in Canada by
Firefly Books Ltd.
66 Leek Crescent
Richmond Hill, Ontario L4B 1H1

Cover and interior design by Bob Wilcox
Front cover photo: Matthias Breiter/Minden Pictures

Printed in China

The publisher gratefully acknowledges the financial support for our publishing program by the Canada Council for the Arts, the Ontario Arts Council and the Government of Canada through the Book Publishing Industry Development Program.

Acknowledgments

Books are always the product of the combined efforts of many. I hope those not mentioned will forgive me their omission. By no means should my failure to list everyone be interpreted as a lack of appreciation; rather it is testimony to my forgetfulness and to space limitations. Without the assistance of John Rogers and Chuck Keim my extended sojourns on the Katmai Coast would have been impossible. Tony Lara provided invaluable assistance and friendship in and around Kodiak. Dean Andrew and Willy Hall got me out to the bears so many times through all kinds of weather. Robert Ponté kept my mobile home running reliably. Missy Epping and Jim Gavin got me home from a photo shoot in Brooks Camp in time for my daughter's birth. Robert Sabin provided accommodation in his cabin in Minnesota while I was photographing black bears. Colette Fontaine, with Travel Manitoba, and Lawreen and Mike Spence made it possible for me to use Watchee Lodge near Churchill as a base to observe newborn polar bear cubs and their moms. Deborah Schildt and Murray Bartholomew provided logistical support and partnership out bush. My thanks also extend to Calvin Riddle for his friendship and to Kent Fredrickson, the ideal person to camp with.

Above all I am indebted to my wife, Laurel Snyder, who is a limitless source of encouragement and patience, even when I again depart for a prolonged trip to the bears. She endured hours of proofreading with a smile. And, last but not least, I am thankful to my daughter Aislyn, who called me home with her early arrival before the weather turned too nasty.

In memory of
Renata Maria Breiter
who always believed in me

Contents

Preface

What good is a bear? The question took me by surprise. I had been thumbing a ride out of Glacier National Park in Montana. After a few weeks in the bush working on a study project, I had run low on supplies and was heading into town to restock. Traffic on the road was light, but the second car stopped for me. Within minutes of getting into the vehicle I found myself in a heated debate over wildlife conservation. As a wildlife biologist I was no stranger to such discussions, so I felt prepared and comfortable in presenting conclusive arguments in favor of environmental protection. Yet this simple query stopped me cold. Since I was trained in the subject matter, I surmised that I should be able to provide a concise, persuasive answer. All that I finally came up with was a vague, drawn-out response that lacked conviction.

The driver of the vehicle wanted to attach a monetary value to the existence of bears. My decision to commit to studying the world's flora and fauna had been based on a deeply felt love for wilderness and the environment. I was enamored of the mysteries of the natural world. A desire to understand the intricacies of nature compelled me to devour any book on the subject. My curiosity was directed toward answering questions such as how an animal or plant grows and survives; how its body is structured; how on a molecular level complex chemical processes result in the procreation, growth, continuance and, ultimately, death of an organism. It hadn't occurred to me to question the purpose of life forms from an economic perspective.

In my opinion, the mere fact that a creature exists gives it a right to live, but this belief is not shared by everyone. Business interests, political agendas and conservation issues conflict regularly; a deep gulf separates the objectives and values of those who represent the various sides. With common ground often a preciously small commodity, the arguments are frequently rich in polemic while communication between the parties remains poor. Symptomatic of this phenomenon is a statement by former governor of Alaska Wally Hickel, who noted on the issue of predator control, "You can't just let nature run wild."

Ever since that car ride, the question about the value of bears has haunted me. In the search for an answer I discovered that there are in fact many reasons for their preservation. As our understanding of interdependencies between species has grown, it has become possible to measure the economic

FACING PAGE: **A young brown bear in Alaska's Katmai National Park keeps a watchful eye on his surroundings as he thirstily slurps up water. His first year of independence is a time of many dangers.**

significance of intact ecosystems. Recent research has revealed that as much as 70 percent of the nitrogen in trees of the Pacific coast temperate rain forest has its origin in the oceans. It is the salmon that brings the richness of the sea to the land, and it is the bear and the eagle that spread the wealth of its nutrients for miles on either side of streams. The forest industry benefits from this fertilization. And healthy trees stabilize mountainsides and provide conditions for the clear, oxygen-rich waters that become nurseries for the salmon, which in its turn is one of the pillars of commercial fishing along the West Coast.

Bears are carnivores. While in many ways they may not match our image of a typical carnivore (assuming there is such a thing), the three North American bear species do display predatory behavior. Predators, while competing with man for resources, fulfill a very important function in ecosystems by keeping prey populations healthy. In the short term, removal of predators has frequently resulted in a dramatic increase in prey populations, with subsequent economic damage to agriculture and forestry. Unless costly management programs are put in place, the peak in animal numbers is inevitably followed by a population crash.

Tourism in national parks and other protected areas has developed into a major industry, creating billions of dollars in revenue in North America each year. Images of bears have been used widely in promotion of countless ecotourism venues. Today bear viewing is creating more revenue than bear hunting – from a dollar perspective, a live bear is now worth more than a dead bear. Sad as it may seem, dollar value is a powerful argument in conservation.

Other aspects of bears' existence are more difficult to quantify in monetary terms. Bears have unknowingly saved many lives and have improved the quality of life for people suffering from chronic diseases. Research into bear physiology has had a major impact on human medicine, specifically in the fields of organ transplants, kidney disease and osteoporosis. Recently biologists have expressed much concern over the dramatic loss of biodiversity. Bears are a prime example of how answers to questions that affect all humankind can be found in nature. If all the bears had disappeared, vital information would have been lost to us forever.

We, both as individual beings and as a society, are the product of our surroundings and our past. This past includes, whether we realize it or not, bears. Bears penetrate human culture, from language to science to art, like no other animal. *Burial*, going *berserk*, to *bear* young – to name but a few – all have etymological roots in the Indo-Germanic word *bher*, the bear. Bears are prominent figures in myths, fairy tales and literature, from North American First Nations' oral traditions to the Grimm brothers and J.R.R. Tolkien. Star constellations are named after the animal.

The threads of history interweave the fabric onto which we embroider the patterns of culture. Societies unravel when individual links with the past are severed. Ignoring our own traditions destabilizes the foundation on which we build the present. Without the bear we lose more than simply a magnificent animal – we irreversibly and irretrievably lose a part of who we are.

In general our society is orphaned from nature. Yet our most creative minds draw inspiration from the natural environment. Cultural diversity is mankind's greatest treasure and asset. Plurality is the spice of life, fostering inspiration and encouraging us to reevaluate old paths and explore new ones. To what degree do we stifle ourselves and our development as people by allowing wilderness to be paved over, tilled into pastures and buried underneath housing developments and malls? By doing so, we rob the great bears of a place to live. To most of us, mountains appear loftier, valleys deeper and forests more mystical in the presence of these majestic creatures. Bears have been called the miner's canary of the wilderness. Because of their large size, they require vast tracts of land on which to live, and are among the first species to disappear if conditions degrade.

Bears have fascinated mankind for millennia. They captivate us today just as they did our ancestors. The good of a bear can be measured in many ways. Yes, a dollar value can be attached to its existence. But while its spiritual and cultural value is much less tangible, it is by no means less significant. In North America we are fortunate to share our country still with these awe-inspiring creatures. Grizzlies, black bears and polar bears have all lost part of their former ranges. Where bears still roam, a fragile truce often prevails between man and beast. Usually it is the people rather than the bear that lack the ability to adapt. Humankind's fears and uneasiness – which find their expression in intolerance – are rooted not so much in what the animals do but in our perception of what they might do. Understanding is the first step to conservation and peaceful coexistence. Only through knowledge can we avoid conflict, recognize their needs and learn to fully appreciate these monarchs of the wilderness. Their future is in our hands.

Matthias Breiter

Introduction

The cool morning breeze whispers in the leaves and ripples the water's surface in the wide cove. The first light of day caresses the tops of tall white pines overlooking the wide expanse of the lake. Underneath the trees, moss and lichen carpet the ground as if wrapping the shallow soil in a warm blanket. This is a land of rocks and trees, a country laced with lakes and rivers. White veins of quartz paint patterns in the grey granite. The surface of the stone has been worn down by time and planed smooth by glaciers that retreated thousands of years in the past.

As the warming sun's rays slide down the trunk of a tree, they touch upon the figure of a black bear. An adult male sits on a limb 30 feet (10 m) from the ground. He reaches out for a branch heavily loaded with pinecones, bends the bough toward him and tenderly plucks off a cone. The bear rolls the cone between his teeth to release the nuts within, spitting out the husks and swallowing the nutritious seeds. Unhurriedly the animal consumes every last tasty morsel, then sits back. His glance rests for a moment on the land spreading below him. This is his home and has been the home of his ancestors from time immemorial. The American black bear is found from the forests of the Florida swamps to the open woodland of the semiarid Southwest, from the oak- and chestnut-covered valleys and ridges of the Appalachians to the rain forest of the Pacific coast. But his stronghold is the northern boreal forest, a belt of continuous woods stretching from Labrador to Alaska. About 450,000 American black bears live in North America, more than the combined population of all other bear species put together.

Over a thousand miles to the north under a turquoise sky, barren mountains tower above dark water on the south side of Devon Island in the Canadian High Arctic. Like white ships without sails, isolated remnants of pack ice drift with the current on Lancaster Sound. When biologists speak of these waters, it is often with the hushed voice of deference. Lancaster Sound is referred to as an Arctic oasis, an area where wildlife abounds, where whales, walrus and seals congregate. Hundreds of thousands of seabirds such as thick-billed murres and black-legged kittiwakes appear every spring to take advantage of the rich resources and raise their young here. Northern fulmars crowd rock ledges at Cape Liddon, their breeding colony stretching for miles.

Down below, at the ocean's edge, inundated by the incessant chuckling, grunting and guttural cries of the birds, lies a juvenile polar bear on a bed of kelp. He has dug himself a comfortable daybed. His head resting on his front feet, he faces the ocean. In contrast to his distant cousin farther south, he hasn't eaten in three weeks. Over much of their range, late summer and fall are a time of slim pickings for polar bears. Their realm is the sea ice. It is there that they hunt for seal and

14

other marine mammals. However, in many places the Arctic Ocean is not ice-covered year-round, stranding the bears on shore for a few weeks or even several months. Land-bound, the animals bed down to live off their fat reserves and conserve energy.

Far to the west, the land lies captive under brooding clouds. From the Gulf of Alaska, the cradle of storms, gales hurl sheets of rain against the coast. This is a virgin country, young and dynamic, ever changing. Invisible on most days, the perfect cone of a volcano, its upper half wrapped in ice and snow, towers above a broad bay. Alder thickets smother the lowlands and envelop the mountainsides. Animal trails form tunnels through the tangled web of branches. They join up, then split again to form a vast labyrinth of passageways through this almost impenetrable mesh of vegetation. An open meadow carpeted with sedges extends between the alder brush and a belt of undulating beach dunes covered in fireweed. White cotton tufts have replaced the crimson petals that weeks before had turned the low parallel ridges into a sea of purple-red. A small, shallow river winds its way through the grassy flats toward the ocean.

On the river's edge sits a female brown bear staring intensely at the water flowing by. Three seven-month-old cubs cuddle against her chocolate-brown bulk. Suddenly she tenses and stands up. Not 10 feet (3 m) out a dorsal fin has broken the water's surface, then vanished again. As the fin reappears above the surface, the female explodes into action. She races into the water and lunges forward with her front legs stretched out. Her head vanishes in the white foam at the base of a large boulder midstream. Moments later she lifts a large chum salmon out of the water and returns to shore, noisily greeted by her excited progeny.

• • •

North America is home to three species of bear, each occupying its own biological niche. The black bear is primarily a denizen of the forest. The polar bear is superbly adapted to life on the sea ice. The grizzly or brown bear evolved on open terrain and uses stands of trees mainly for shelter. The diet of black bears and brown bears consists of as much as 80 percent vegetable matter, whereas polar bears are almost exclusively predatory. Yet as different as they are, a common thread links all three species – there is no one truth about their habitat, food source or range.

Boundaries blur as the animals explore their limits. Black bears, although their diet is dominated by plants for much of the year, prey heavily on new-born deer calves. In some areas over 40 percent of moose calves fall victim to grizzlies. In part of their range polar bears feed on berries in the summer. Before the demise of the fish runs from over-harvesting, seventeenth-century reports tell of polar bears congregating at salmon streams on the Labrador coast. In recent decades the black bear has extended its range to include the open tundra of the Ungava Peninsula in northeastern Canada, because the grizzly was hunted to extinction there in the early twentieth century. These bears live their lives hundreds of miles north of the tree line. In spring, grizzly bears have been seen hunting for seals on the sea ice 60 miles (100 km) from land. Anyone making absolute statements about bears is invariably, sooner or later, proven wrong by these animals.

Bears are generalists and opportunists; they are intelligent and learn quickly. This combination of traits embodies the essence of bears. It enables the animals to adjust to a vast range of environmental conditions. The success of this survival strategy is reflected in their flexible diet and in their range. Of all mammal species, the brown bear has the largest distribution, covering almost 18,000 miles (29,000 km), from northern Spain to the western shores of Hudson Bay and Yellowstone National Park in Wyoming. The polar bear is found throughout the entire Arctic, from Spitsbergen and eastern Greenland to the Canadian High Arctic and eastern Russia. The American black bear lives in every Canadian province except for Prince Edward Island, and in at least 32 states.

All living bear species, eight in total, are to some degree opportunists, utilizing food sources as they become available. Even the highly specialized panda will occasionally add some carrion to its diet of bamboo. Neither does the sloth bear solely eat insects. In the taxonomic system, bears belong to the carnivores. Anatomical, serological and paleontological evidence leave no doubt of that. Based on their diets, however, with the exception of the polar bears the animals don't match our perception of a carnivore, a meat-eater. The term is misleading to start with, as the act of eating meat is not decisive in determining the taxonomic status of an animal. Numerous mammals that are not carnivores nevertheless add meat to their diet. Many rodents are opportunistically carnivorous, and even a herbivore may occasionally eat a vertebrate. Caribou, for instance, have been observed consuming lemmings.

Our idea of what a carnivore is supposed to be is based on animals such as cats and dogs. Yet the order Carnivora, to which cats and dogs and all other carnivores belong, comprises a physically variable group of mammals – 254 species in total. Apart from terrestrial carnivores it also includes the aquatic pinnipeds, or finfeet, which include species such as sea lions, walrus and seals.

The suborder Fissipedia, in which all terrestrial carnivores are lumped together, consists of seven families: Canidae (dogs), Felidae (cats), Procyonidae (raccoons), Mustelidae (weasels), Viverridae (mongooses), Hyaenidae (hyenas) and, last but not least, Ursidae (bears). In defiance of this taxonomic arrangement, which tries to group together what is most closely related, the pinnipeds are apparently, after the raccoons, the bear's next of kin within the Carnivora.

The diversity of animals included in the order Carnivora also finds expression in their size. The smallest, the least weasel, weighs a mere 2 ounces (50 g), whereas the largest terrestrial carnivore, an adult male polar or brown bear, tips the scale at over 1,500 pounds (700 kg), 1,400 times the weight of the least weasel. A southern sea elephant is heavier yet, reaching four tons in weight.

Common to all carnivores is their evolutionary lineage. They can all trace their heritage back to the same ancestors, the miacids, which lived 60 to 70 million years ago. Many species (such as the cats) diverged quickly from a more herbivorous diet toward eating meat. Bears, on the other hand, represent the opposite trend toward a more generalized food source. The ability to switch between food sources, from a herbivorous to a carnivorous diet depending on availability, is unique to the bears. This flexibility has proven to be a very successful foraging concept, particularly in a temperate climate, which has seasonal abundance of resources.

The first true bear-like carnivore was *Ursavus*, a fox-sized forest dweller that lived in Eurasia 25 million years ago, in an epoch of geological history called the Miocene. *Ursavus* gave rise to two different lineages: *Agriotherium* and *Indarctos*. *Indarctos* took a more herbivorous route, which culminated in one of the few almost exclusively vegetarian carnivores, the giant panda. *Agriotherium*, on the other hand, developed to fill a more predatory niche and eventually diverged into two branches, the Tremarctinae, or short-faced bears, and the Ursinae, the so-called true bears. The Tremarctinae were the first bears to reach the New World 15 million years ago. In the Pliocene they became extinct in their ancestral home in Eurasia, yet they thrived in America, evolving into two genera, *Tremarctos* and *Arctodus*. The latter included the species *Arctodus simus*, the giant short-faced bear.

Two wolves and a grizzly share the remains of a moose that the wolves brought down earlier. Although 80 percent of a grizzly's diet consists of vegetable matter, a large carcass represents an opportunity to feast that is too tempting to resist. It will compete fervently for access to the rich food source.

In the Pleistocene (from two million to 10,000 years ago), the giant short-faced bear was the largest and most powerful predator in the world. An adult male weighed one ton. Remains of this formidable beast have been unearthed in deposits containing human artifacts, suggesting that Paleo-Indians coexisted for a short time with this super-predator before it disappeared at the end of the last ice age. Climate change and an associated shift in vegetation patterns, possibly aggravated by human hunting pressure, caused the large prey the animal depended upon to die out. With its food source gone, the giant short-faced bear became extinct as well. The Tremarctinae are not yet, however, a dead branch on the tree of evolution. One member survives into the present – the spectacled bear, which hangs on tenaciously in the northern and central Andes of South America.

The Ursinae eventually gave rise to the remaining six modern bear species. All of them are members of the genus *Ursus*, which first appeared in the Pliocene in western Eurasia. From there they expanded their realm and eventually, about 3.5 million years ago, reached North America. From this ancestral stock rose the American black bear. As a late arrival, the black bear had to contend with the giant short-faced bear as the supreme predator in open country. The unoccupied niche was that of a primarily arboreal forest dweller. Trees provided an escape route, safe habitat and food.

Defending resources or cubs against superior predators is effectively suicide; animals that stood their ground in a confrontation more often than
not would have been killed. As a result, today's American black bears are
genetically predisposed to retreat and flee rather than to fight when threatened. It is a testimony to the plasticity of bear behavior – and possibly the
speed at which evolutionary processes can operate when new doors open –
that the population of black bears that spread onto the treeless tundra of
the Ungava Peninsula apparently act more aggressively than their cousins
farther south. Their response to a threat takes a leaf out of the grizzly's book
of behavioral etiquette.

The lineage that produced the American black bear also produced the
bears of the Old World. The present-day sun bear, sloth bear and Asiatic
black bear are the result of this speciation process.

The late Pliocene was a period of dramatic, widespread and often relatively
rapid climatic change. The world slipped into a series of ice ages. During a
cooling trend, average animal size increases, and the bears were no exception. They grew larger and a new species arose in Eurasia, *Ursus etruscus*,
which in the mid-Pleistocene (about 1.6 million years ago) evolved into the
modern brown bear, probably in Western Europe. By 800,000 years ago it
had expanded eastward. Recent DNA data suggests that brown bears

TOP: **The long jaws of a brown bear contain large cusped molars needed to crush vegetable food. The carnassials – the fourth upper premolar and first lower molar, which slice meat – are reduced.**

BOTTOM: **By comparison, the teeth of a fox are sharper and better suited to mincing meat than to chewing plant material.**

inhabited the vast plains of Beringia, which now lie submerged below the Bering Sea, and crossed into Alaska 50,000 to 70,000 years ago.

A population was able to establish itself along the coastal islands of southeastern Alaska and western British Columbia. However, at that point their progress stalled. For thousands of years brown bears remained restricted to Alaska and the northwest coast of the New World. The reasons were probably twofold. The Cordilleran and Laurentian ice sheets blocked the inland route into more southerly regions, and in the prevailing drier and colder climate, a broad belt of grasslands dominated the land immediately south of the ice. The open country was the domain of the giant short-faced bear, which was quite likely too much of a predator for the smaller brown bear to coexist with. As the glaciers receded about 13,000 years ago, the Mackenzie Corridor opened a migration path between the coastal and inland ice sheets to southern Canada and the lower 48 states. The climate became warmer and more humid, the grasslands shrank and the forests extended their range. The dynasty of the giant short-faced bear faded, to be replaced by a new monarch – the grizzly.

The most recent bear species to appear on the global stage of biodiversity is the polar bear. Probably about 200,000 to 300,000 years ago a population of brown bears became isolated by advancing ice sheets and inhospitable terrain on the north coast of eastern Siberia. Lacking other food, they started to utilize the rich marine resources available and adapted to life on the pack ice. From there they quickly spread across the Arctic. The oldest fossil of a true polar bear is less than 100,000 years old and was found, of all places, near the Kew Bridge in London, England. It is unclear when the first polar bear reached the North American continent. The probable location is northwestern Alaska, in an area now drowned by rising sea levels. Quite likely they also frequented the northeastern seaboard in times when that area was part of the southern extent of the annual pack ice. Over much of today's Canadian Arctic the animal wasn't present earlier than 10,000 years ago, as ice sheets almost 2 miles (3 km) thick held the land captive until then.

The first encounter between mankind and the bear will always remain hidden behind the veil of prehistory. When humans appeared on the scene, extending their range out of Africa into the realm of the bear, today's species had already occupied their niche for many thousands of generations. The impact on the bear would have been major from the very start; a competitor with almost identical food requirements had suddenly emerged. People ate the same plants and supplemented their diet with animals they killed or scavenged on, just like bears. They used the same habitat – what looked good to a bear looked just as appealing to early humans. They became cohabitants of an ecological niche. In Europe, the cave bear and people even competed for shelter.

The bears for the most part were identical to the animals we know today. Mankind, however, was quite different physically and even more so culturally. The earliest contact would have been between Neanderthal people and bears. Later, modern man, the Cro-Magnon, followed. Both the Neanderthal people and the Cro-Magnon lived in hunter-gatherer societies. Band size was small. A clan consisted of several families, as otherwise the scattered resources would be exploited too quickly. People lived as semi-nomads in order to make use of food as it became available locally. They were intimately familiar with the flora and fauna that they shared the land with – their survival depended on it. In-depth knowledge of animals that could be threats, food sources or competitors was paramount for them to master the vicissitudes of nature. Bears, their idiosyncrasies, behavioral traits and annual life cycle were thus well-known.

Hunter-gatherer societies perceive their surroundings very differently than we do. Their social system has little in the way of hierarchy. Leadership is mostly nonhereditary and dependent on the abilities of the individual. And as abilities can change, so can status. Division of labor is minimal and mostly gender-specific. There is no surplus production to allow parts of society to forsake hunting, collecting or procuring food. Everyone is a generalist in an egalitarian society. And the social structure of society extends into the metaphysical. Every part of their environment, be it animals, plants or features of the landscape, is interwoven into a cohesive fabric that forms both the material and the spiritual world. Geological features have creation stories attached to them. Frequently they are the resting-places of creator beings or powerful spirits. Each living thing and object possesses a malevolent or benevolent spirit, a belief we now call animism. Animals are regarded as equals endowed with human capabilities, if not supernatural powers.

As dwellers in the Western world, we have become spectators of the natural environment rather than participants. We are removed from the fight for survival by well-insulated homes, supermarkets and a social welfare system. We are the products of our times and the world we live in. Inevitably, compared to a hunter-gatherer society, our perception of nature is more distant or, one might say, more objective. Yet, when observing bears, even we have a tendency to anthropomorphize the animal. Many of their behavioral characteristics appear fundamentally human. Their young and juveniles are playful and boisterous, curious and mischievous, gentle and rough. They display capabilities of problem solving and learning. Their character is shaped by their experiences, and as the experiences of individuals vary, so does their character. Some bears are timid, others daring; some are friendly and tolerant toward people, others have an attitude. We admire the devotion a female displays toward her offspring. We value her strong protective traits in the face of danger, even against overwhelming odds.

Brown bears congregate along freshwater streams during the salmon run. Over much of history, bears and man have competed over seasonally abundant food sources and prime habitat, resulting in displacement of the animals from much of their range.

In addition, anatomical characteristics make us feel akin to bears. They are the only mammals apart from humans and apes that walk on the soles of their feet. Other attributes are not as apparent to us but would have been familiar to early humans. For instance, a skinned bear carcass looks eerily like a human body. Part of the bear's life cycle would have added to the animal's mystique. In late fall, bears retreat into dens to pass the long winter months in deep sleep, motionless – seeming to walk, if not actually cross, the boundary between life and death – only to reappear in spring when the land rejuvenates. Adult females enter the den alone, showing no indication of carrying new life, and reemerge accompanied by cubs, seeming living proof of the miracle of virgin birth. Not surprisingly, more than any other animal, bears were held in great honor by all pre-agrarian societies. Bears were perceived to be able to communicate with the spirit world, to travel thither and return at will. They were seen as messengers through whom contact could be established with people who had passed on to the afterlife. Bears became the central element in fertility rites. Some societies glorified them as gods.

This spiritual relationship with the bear can be traced back to the dawn of humankind. In a cave in Switzerland archaeologists found an altar-like stone slab erected by Neanderthal people over 50,000 years ago. Seven bear skulls were arranged upon it, all facing the entrance of the cavern. At Regourdou, in France, a Neanderthal gravesite contained the arm bone of

a cave bear. In other places, buried bodies were covered with pieces of bear fur. Possibly the Neanderthals associated the bear with rebirth and the afterlife. The oldest depiction dates back 30,000 years. In Péchialet, in the Dordogne (France), Paleolithic people engraved deeply into a rock wall the images of two men dancing with a bear.

Bears continued to enchant and mesmerize people as they started to settle in villages. The Vinca culture, which flourished 5,000 to 9,000 years ago, left behind bear-shaped cult vases and terracotta figurines in the form of a bear-headed woman, often shown nursing a cub. Several thousand years later, a bear cult flourished in Greece. Trophonios, a cave-dwelling oracle, traced his lineage back to the bear. In Greek mythology the animal also found its way into the sky. As punishment, Zeus set Callisto and Arcas into the heavens as Ursa Major and Ursa Minor, the Great Bear and the Little Bear. Interestingly, the Inuit people, who have no cultural link whatsoever to the society of classical Greece, also associate the constellation of Ursa Major with the bear and have their own myth about the placing of the animal among the stars.

North American First Nations can provide us with insight into the degree to which bears penetrated cultures that were pre-agrarian or had limited agriculture, as their oral traditions are still alive. Many First Nations, all across the continent, regarded bears as essentially fur-clad people. Belief that the animal could temporarily slip out of its coat and walk

Cooling off by dissipating heat through his arm and leg pits, a polar bear relaxes spread-eagled on the ice. Polar bear numbers were in steep decline and threatened by increased hunting pressure until the five polar bear nations – Canada, U.S.A., Denmark, Norway and the USSR – signed a landmark agreement in 1973 on the protection of the animals and their habitat.

about as man, unrecognized, was widespread. The Tlingit along southeast Alaska's coast considered brown bears to be half-human. The Ojibwa called bears *anijinabe*, their word for themselves. The Blackfoot term *o-kits-kits* refers to both the human hand and a bear's paw. The Cree called the grizzly Chief's Son; the Navajo referred to him as Fine Young Chief. Also common in many Native American groups were the names Cousin, Grandfather and Elder Brother.

As human civilization shifted from a seminomadic hunter-gatherer existence to an economy based on agriculture, man's attitude toward and relationship with the natural world, including bears, began to change. Increasingly the animals were seen as competition and vermin. Worship and adoration turned to dislike, if not outright hatred. Man began to see predators in the most fiendish colors. His loss of image would hardly have bothered the bear. However, he was no match for the destructive ingenuity of humankind, which exhibits its potential to the fullest whenever an obstacle has to be removed or an enemy annihilated.

Armed with high-handed self-righteousness and a sense of civic duty, men hounded bears with dogs, ran arrows and lances through their bodies, destroyed their innards with poison bait, and blasted them with bullets from muskets, pistols and rifles. Yet humans weren't satisfied with simply exterminating the bear. The animal was put on display, imprisoned in cages for the amusement of the public. The Romans, obsessed with the idea of imposing human order and control over the savageness of nature, included beasts such as lions and bears in circus performances, where they were pitted against fellow beasts, gladiators, prisoners and soldiers. The emperor Commodus shot a hundred brown bears with arrows in one event. Under the rule of Gordian a thousand bears were used over the course of a single "games." The use of bears for entertainment of the masses continued into more recent times. In California between 1816 and 1880, for instance, fights were staged between bears and bulls.

Thus the future of bears in the world of humans looked bleak. They could only emerge out of the conflict defeated. If they didn't get killed, habitat destruction robbed them of the basis for survival; the final result was the same. In Western Europe, the last bear in England was shot in the eleventh century, and in Germany, in the nineteenth century. A few shy individuals survive in the Pyrenees of northern Spain and in central Italy. While protected now, their population numbers are so low that extinction appears to be only a matter of time unless they receive a helping hand.

The first bears that the European settlers in the New World encountered were black bears. However, to the surprise of many, they weren't the only species. In the late sixteenth century polar bears were apparently common along the Labrador coast, the Gulf of St. Lawrence and the shores of Newfoundland. By the late seventeenth century they were already rare in the most southern reaches of their former distribution because of persecution for food and fur, and out of a conviction that any large carnivore should be destroyed whenever possible. In the late eighteenth century they were still recorded in great numbers along salmon streams on the Labrador coast. But by then whalers working that coastline were killing every white bear they could find and trading for pelts with the Labrador Inuit. By 1850 few bears were to be seen on that coast. Today a polar bear is spotted in the Gulf of St. Lawrence only occasionally, arriving in the spring aboard an ice floe carried south by the Labrador Current.

The black bear abounded along the eastern seaboard and in forested areas all across the country. The early colonists slaughtered them for food and fur, and because they saw them as a threat to agriculture. Whereas the Native population viewed the animal mostly with respect and reverence, the new arrivals reserved their admiration for those who killed the beasts. They were seen as saviors of settlements and homes. The likes of Daniel Boone, who massacred as many as two thousand black bears, and Davy Crockett, who killed 105 in the winter of 1825–26 alone, were considered heroes.

When Lewis and Clark crossed the western part of the American continent between 1804 and 1806, both black and brown bears were shot for food whenever the opportunity arose. The explorers' journal entries tell of encounters with grizzlies along the Missouri River on an almost daily basis. Their reports were the basis for the original scientific description of the animal, by George Ord in 1815, who assigned it the designation *Ursus horribilis*, the "horrible bear." Ord, who had never seen a grizzly, depicted the animal as "the enemy of man" that "literally thirsts for human blood. So far from shunning, he [the grizzly] seldom fails to attack; and even to hunt him." The journals of Lewis and Clark, consumed by the public without critical analysis and embellished, distorted and misinterpreted by authors and authorities such as Ord, influenced the perceptions of several generations. Then, as now, a good story involved drama and depicted brave people fighting a righteous battle against vicious beasts in an unforgiving country. A bear that showed fear of humans or ignored the new interlopers, unless provoked and attacked first, would have portrayed reality – but didn't sell as well. Even today, books about bear attacks outperform volumes written in a more conciliatory tone.

After Lewis and Clark had long since returned to the East, between roughly 1840 and 1900, when the West was conquered and settled by waves of Euro-Americans, the grizzly epitomized the evil wilderness. Killing the beast was part of the job that had to be done to civilize the country. Aided by new rifles that were vastly superior to those Lewis and Clark had to rely upon – which nowadays would be considered totally inappropriate to tackle a grizzly with – men didn't take long to push the great bear into oblivion on the prairies. Well before the turn of the century the grizzly had made its last stand in Kansas, Nebraska, South Dakota, Oklahoma, Texas and Manitoba. In North Dakota a brown bear was shot in the fall of 1897; no others have been reported since. Farther west, in California, Arizona, New Mexico, Utah and Oregon, grizzlies survived in remnant populations until the 1920s and early 1930s. In the lower 48 states the great bear has vanished from 99 percent of its former range. The smaller and more adaptable black bears faired better, their distribution restricted by "only" 50 percent.

Sparked by a mounting disenchantment with growing industrialization, Romanticism swept through Europe in the early and mid-nineteenth century before jumping the Atlantic. A strong interest in nature and a revolt against blind adherence to traditions and rules typified the new thinking. The rule of reason was replaced by an emphasis on emotion. In North America, Henry David Thoreau expressed these sentiments in *Walden* and in his essay *Civil Disobedience*. Thoreau stood at the forefront of a rapidly changing view of our relationship with nature and wild places. He was followed by the likes of John Muir, Theodore Roosevelt, Bob Marshall, Aldo Leopold, and Olaus and Adolph Murie. They were key players in the evolution of the idea of wildlife conservation and the role of a responsible nation in protecting the environment and its denizens. In little more than a hundred years the bear was transformed from a symbol of everything perceived evil in nature – that which must be destroyed – to the figurehead of a fight for protection of our wild heritage. We are now more inclined to find fault in the human victim of a bear mauling than in the bear.

Despite having recognized the value of wild places and of bears, we are still far from accepting the animals as part of our local environment. Their perceived rightful place is in untouched, remote wilderness areas, locations that we can enter at will or stay away from if we choose to. Nature has been given the role of an adventure theme park, a place where we try to get in touch with our inner self, find peace and fulfill some desire to be one with the environment. After we leave, however, we reveal our alienation by denying wildlife a place to live outside the invisible boundaries of designated wilderness areas. As soon as a bear is spotted near homes and farms it transforms into a potential threat to life and property. Our tolerance diminishes in proportion to the distance between the beast and our private sphere, and evaporates when the animal is perceived to trespass on personal interests. The problem is mounting as wilderness areas become habitat islands in a landscape fragmented by human activity.

The grizzly is particularly affected by this trend. About a thousand brown bears still live in the lower 48 states, down from an estimated 150,000 animals in 1800. The population in the Yellowstone ecosystem, although healthy at over three hundred individuals, is isolated. The same is true for the few remaining brown bears in the Selkirk Mountains in Idaho and the Cabinet Mountains on the Montana–Idaho border. In national parks throughout the western United States, as well as in other parts of the world, large mammals vanished within decades of establishment of the protected areas. The parks were simply not large enough to support viable populations.

It has been shown that about a hundred breeding females are required to guarantee the survival of a population for the next hundred years. In the case of bears, this translates into a total population of 300 to 400 animals. By this calculation the Yellowstone population is in good shape for the immediate future. The populations in the Selkirk and Cabinet mountains, however, are doomed unless bears can migrate from outlying areas to keep the gene pool healthy and compensate for accidental deaths. The establishment of habitat corridors along which animals can disperse is thus of major significance, and several conservation agencies are fighting for them.

Black bear populations in the southeastern United States face similar problems of habitat fragmentation. The loss of habitat due to logging or housing developments sometimes results in bears searching for alternate food sources, and they find them in orchards, in fruit trees in people's backyards and in garbage dumps. The increased number of "bear incidents" gives the impression that the bear population has grown, when in fact it is in steep decline. Residential areas and garbage dumps act as population sinks. The bears' mortality rate is high and reproduction almost nonexistent. In Banff National Park in Alberta, the black bear population was considered healthy

FACING PAGE: A juvenile black bear rests high in a tree, safe from larger bears and other predators. While displaced from 50 percent of its former range, the black bear is still by far the most abundant and widespread bear in North America, occurring in at least 32 states and in every Canadian province but Prince Edward Island.

as recently as the 1980s. This assessment was based in part on the high frequency of problem bears near the town of Banff. Between 1950 and 1980 wardens in Banff and Jasper national parks killed more than 523 black bears and moved an additional 547 animals. A study then revealed that only 20 black bears remained in the Bow River Valley.

There is hope. Because of stringent hunting regulations and their strict enforcement, bear populations are stable over most of North America. Over the past few decades, several areas with high bear density have been put under protection. Some of them have become tourist magnets where we are given the opportunity to establish a new relationship with the animal. Although a rat's nest of problems accompanies an increase in popularity, this development gives rise to optimism. These natural wonderlands, in which the protection of bears takes precedence over the interests of people, teach us that it is possible to live in harmony with the beast if rules of conduct are observed and respect for the animal is shown.

Very often it takes only small changes to avoid conflict and achieve big results. In logging areas in the Pacific Northwest, black bears were causing substantial damage to tree plantations. In the spring, when few other food sources are available, bears strip the bark off young trees to feed on the cambium layer beneath. Under natural conditions the damage is small, as young trees tend to be scattered thinly throughout the forest. But in a human-made environment, replanting efforts were being foiled. Logging companies found it cheaper and less controversial to provide the bears with an alternative food source for a few weeks rather than trying to eliminate the animals. As soon as the land began to green up, the problem was alleviated as the bears left for richer pastures.

Beekeepers have started putting solar-powered electric fences around their hives to keep bears out. This method also works well for protecting cottages in late fall, before the animals den up. Putting garbage out for pickup in the morning instead of the night before represents a small change in our behavior, but protects bears by not habituating them to human food. And storing dog food out of reach of bears is just another step toward peaceful coexistence.

Ours is the advantage, and not just because of our superior weapons and greater numbers. We cannot expect bears to adapt to us – they are unable to see the world from a human perspective. Bears do whatever they have to do to survive in their world. But we are able to put ourselves in the bears' position, to perceive the world through their eyes and, with small changes in our habits and behavior, to share the land with these magnificent beasts without getting into conflict. This takes goodwill and tolerance. It requires educating people to understand the way of the bear. But coexistence is within our means and in our hands. It is simply a question of resolve.

February

Chapter One

A New Life Is Born

Rolling hills stretch to the horizon under an azure sky. Their high-arched backs are covered by the bald dark bodies of red and white oak interspersed with hemlocks, cedars and majestic white pines. In the creek bottoms, silver maples thrive. A thick blanket of snow covers the ground. At the base of a steep slope an old deer track winds among the trees and passes by the huge trunk of a mature red oak before climbing the hillside. In winter nature speaks in hushed voices. The trickle of water, the rush of a creek, the murmur of a river are frozen until the thaw of spring, still months away. However, during the shortest months of the year the flame of life is not extinguished. It often burns low to conserve energy, but in some instances it shines brightly but secretly, hidden from view.

A fox follows the twisting course of the deer track, avoiding the deep snow. When he reaches the red oak he stops and sniffs the bark. Old claw marks lead up the trunk. But it's not the marks that raise the fox's interest. As he stands next to the tree he can faintly hear a soft whimper. In the dead of winter, new life has begun.

Fifty feet (15 m) above the ground, a small hole barely 16 inches (40 cm) across forms an entry to the hollow center of the tree. At the bottom lies a female black bear on a bed of wood shavings, moss and a few boughs carried in during the fall. The bear is awake. In the twilight of the den, two cubs just minutes old squirm between her front legs. The female has another contraction. A tiny, wet pink body covered in embryonic membranes is welcomed into the world. Its mother turns and picks up her third cub gently between her teeth. After placing it among its siblings, she licks the new arrival thoroughly, freeing it from the membranes and drying its thin fur. Afterward she consumes the afterbirth, then lies back down and curls up.

The curve of the female's body and her folded legs form the walls of a nursing chamber. In the microclimate of this protected pocket, warmed by her body and her breath, the cubs will thrive during the following months. Without this cozy refuge they would freeze to death. Newborn bear cubs are covered in fine hair that offers almost no protection from the cold; in fact, their coat is so light that they appear almost naked. For the first month their eyes are sealed shut. They are deaf and toothless. Their stubby legs cannot support them. In short, they are totally helpless and dependent on their mother for warmth, food and protection. Outside the temperatures sink to −22°F (−30°C) as night falls. In the tree den the temperature hovers around freezing. This is a harsh time to care for a new litter.

· · ·

It looks like one of nature's follies that bears are born during the worst of winter. No other mammal living in the North gives birth at this time. And no other mammals except the marsupials have such immature offspring. Bears have the smallest young in relation to the mother's body size of any higher mammal. Typically bear cubs weigh between one three-hundredth and one five-hundredth as much as their mother. On average a newborn black bear cub weighs little more than 10.5 ounces (300 g) and is 9 inches (23 cm) long. Brown bear and polar bear cubs are marginally larger, about 17.5 to 28 ounces (500–800 g) in weight and 12 inches (30 cm) in length. If a newborn human infant were that small in comparison, it would weigh between 3.6 and 6 ounces (100–170 g), the weight of a 14- to 16-week fetus. Even in the most advanced neonatal intensive care unit, a baby born at such an early developmental stage could not be saved; it would simply not be viable. For bears, on the other hand, the birth of premature cubs is normal – indeed, inevitable.

The bear's evolution toward an omnivorous diet proved a very successful strategy, and bears occupy a vast array of different habitats. However, there is always a price to pay. The animals evolved in a temperate climate with distinct winter periods. While food is abundant seasonally, during the short months of the year very little digestible fare is available to a bear. If more calories are burned in the search for food than are gained by consuming whatever is found, there is little incentive to remain active. The alternative is to slow down the metabolic rate to conserve energy. Consequently most bears spend the winter months in a state of reduced activity; that is, the animals hibernate.

A black bear cub, just weeks old, lies nestled between the front legs of its mother in a sub-terranean birth den. In the northern boreal forest, trees are often too small to serve as a den site. In addition, snow blanketing the land acts as an insulator against the bitter cold.

At an age of one month this Kodiak bear cub opens its eyes for the first time. The white collar around the neck will fade as the animal gets older; it is usually not noticeable in adult animals.

A fasting animal – and hibernation is a prolonged fasting period – burns fat almost exclusively in order to supply the metabolic furnace with the energy required to stay alive. Fat consists of two components: glycerin and fatty acids. Fatty acids are long-chain molecules, and therein lies the problem. The fetus gets its nourishment through the placenta. The placenta is a membrane, and only small molecules can travel through it. Fatty-acid molecules are simply too large. Amino acids, the building blocks of protein, can travel through the placenta. Thus the pregnant female can meet the demands of her unborn young only through breaking down her own body protein. Since the only large source of protein is muscle tissue, ultimately this would put the female's life at risk by melting away her muscle mass. If the female carried the cub to what we consider full term, she would come out of hibernation unable to move her own body. To solve the problem, the period of gestation is shortened and the cubs are born at a premature stage of development.

The cubs continue their growth outside their mother's body, but now they receive their nourishment through milk. For the first few months they rely exclusively on milk for food. Bear milk is extremely rich in order to encourage rapid growth in the cubs. Its protein content is between 11 and 15 percent so that it can provide the essential amino acids for muscle development. The energy the cubs require is now supplied by fat, which they absorb through the digestive system. In black bears and grizzlies the

average fat content of the milk is 22 to 24 percent. In polar bears the mean value for the fat content is even higher, at 33 percent. The highest fat content ever measured was 48 percent.

Considering the high demand for protein during pregnancy, the question arises as to whether bears could avoid the problem by bulking up on protein instead of adding a layer of fat. As it turns out, because of the chemical properties of the compounds, this is not an option. Stored fat contains very little water. Consequently, about two and half times more energy can be derived from a gram of fat than from a gram of carbohydrate (sugars) or protein. If a bear stored its excess energy as protein, the increased mass would interfere with her mobility – she could not even walk to the den site. And to metabolize amino acids, water is required, which is available to a hibernating animal only through the breakdown of fat. Subcutaneous fat reserves are also an efficient insulator, as fat conducts heat only one-third as readily as other tissues.

Other mammals hibernate in the winter, yet have their young in the spring, not in the dead of winter. However, they are all small animals. A mammal's gestation period is linked to its size. It takes time for a fetus to grow from fertilized egg to full-term young. The cell size of mammals is similar, regardless of the body size of the animal, so a larger fetus consists of more cells and consequently takes longer to grow. A small hibernator such as the Arctic ground squirrel or the marmot can emerge from its den in May,

A female grizzly gently sniffs her cub. Bears recognize their young primarily by smell. Cases of misidentification occur when cubs of different mothers mingle at an abundant food source.

37

mate, have its young in early summer and even wean the next generation before the end of the season. A bear is unable to do so. The normal gestation period for an animal of its size is at least nine months. This means that the pregnancy must take place during hibernation.

Hibernation is a response to food shortage, not to low temperatures. In areas where food is available in the winter, some grizzlies and black bears remain active and don't retreat into a den. With the exception of pregnant females, polar bears do not hibernate, as their prey, marine mammals, stay in the Arctic regions year round and the bears hunt them extensively in the winter. This represents another riddle in the reproductive biology of bears. It would appear to be advantageous for a female polar bear to head out onto the ice in the fall and hunt until her time to give birth arrives. The longer feeding period would reduce the physiological stress on her body caused by denning and nursing her newborn cubs. Instead she enters her maternity domicile in September or October and remains in hibernation until her cubs are born, between late November and January. The reason for this apparently irrational behavior lies in a specific feature of bear pregnancy.

The gestation period of all mammals has two stages. After the ovum is fertilized, the zygote splits into blastomeres and continues dividing until it is a spherical sac the size of a pinhead (about 1 or 2 mm in diameter) called a blastocyst. This process takes about a week or so. Further cell divisions cannot take place because all the material the ovum provided has now been used up. In order to grow, the blastocyst has to implant in the uterus wall,

LEFT: **The claw indentations falling far forward of the toes in the bottom print clearly identify these tracks in the snow as those of an adult grizzly.**

RIGHT: **In brown bear cubs the claws are still short and sharp, enabling them to easily scale trees for safety.**

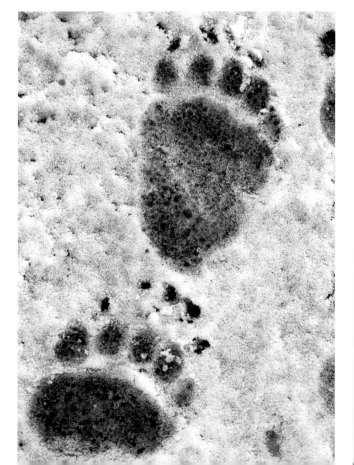

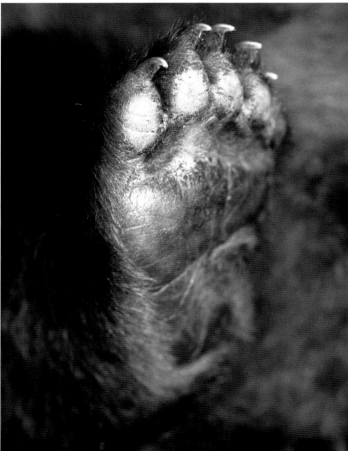

where a placenta develops through which the fetus is nourished. In bears the process ceases after the blastocyst stage is reached, a phenomenon called delayed implantation or embryonic diapause. The blastocyst implants in the wall of the uterus only when the female goes into hibernation. This course of events leaves the polar bear female no choice – she has to go into hibernation or the pregnancy will abort. The blastocyst will not implant if the female remains active. Delayed implantation in polar bears is part of the evolutionary baggage these animals inherited through their brown bear ancestry.

Delayed implantation is found in many groups of mammals, including rodents, bats, seals and deer. It has been described in about a hundred species. Among the carnivores, in addition to bears, it is also widespread in the weasel family. Similar quiescent stages in the development of the embryo occur in kangaroos. The purpose of delayed implantation is to separate the prime feeding times from the mating season. In bears and members of the deer family it also has the advantage that very little is invested in the next generation until the start of winter. If the female is unable to build up sufficient fat reserves over the summer and fall to sustain both her and her fetus and young until spring, the pregnancy is terminated.

Delayed implantation makes it difficult to answer clearly the question of length of gestation in bears. If one includes the time during which development of the embryo is suspended, total gestation in bears is between seven and nine months. Yet the actual period of fetal development is only about two and a half months.

· · ·

Crepuscular gloom replaces darkness in the tree hollow as the sun climbs high above the hills outside. The cubs have nursed every three hours during the night. Now they wake again and move toward their mother's nipples, gently assisted by her paws. They find the source of milk by migrating toward heat. When researchers aimed an infrared camera at a hibernating mother bear, they discovered that she radiated heat from two sources, her muzzle and her nipples. As they latch on and start suckling, the cubs' soft, contented humming fills the den.

Ten minutes later, exhausted from nursing, they fall back asleep. The female licks their bottoms and bellies to stimulate the release of urine and feces. As they void, she licks it up to keep the den clean. When humans first learned about bears thousands of years ago, a widespread idea was that it was the mother's licking that shaped the cubs, because at birth they look more like chubby chipmunks than bruins. As a linguistic remnant, an ill-behaved, incorrigible child in France is still called a badly licked bear.

The female lies back down, gently blowing warm air over her new litter. It will be several months before the cubs see the sun for the first time. The world will be warmer then and the first flowers will be pushing through the moist soil. Silent snow starts falling as the day wanes. Spring is still a distant dream.

March

Chapter Two

A Cold Start

High clouds form a white dome over the coastal lowlands of the southwest shore of Hudson Bay. Along the coast, tundra ecosystems and the scraggly trees of the taiga fight for supremacy over the land. Clusters of white spruce are surrounded by ground-hugging willow bushes. The trees pay levy to the northwesterlies – stripped clean on the windward side, their remaining branches point like a storm-torn flag to the southeast. Inland the force of the Arctic winds is broken where the clusters of spruce merge to form a barrier. The taiga wins the battle. An expanse of forest composed of evergreens, poplars and birch, broken by shallow ponds and the courses of creeks and streams, stretches into the west. Thirty miles (50 km) from the ocean, the meandering course of the Owl River has dug a trench in the sandy soil. On its north side a line of stunted trees, bent by age and climate, stands sentinel over the stream 30 feet (10 m) below.

The Arctic and subarctic are thirsty lands. What little snow falls over the course of winter is driven across the country by the tireless wind. Where the lay of the land creates eddies in the air currents, waves of snow form, their surface polished hard. Here, sloping steeply down toward the frozen river in the lee of the trees, a drift buries the north side of the gully. The surface of this snow dune is broken halfway up by a gaping hole, almost invisible from the bottom, that provides access to its bowl. A female polar bear lies in her daybed next to the opening. Her head, eyes closed, rests on her paws. Although the temperature is –13°F (–25°C), she is enjoying the nap on her balcony.

Three small heads appear in the entrance. Her cubs glance at their mother and whine to get her attention, but when she doesn't react they vanish inside again. Until a few hours ago their entire world was confined to the white and brown walls of their den. They were born three months earlier into a home barely large enough to contain them and their mother. Maternity dens are usually amazingly small. Their purpose is to serve as a sleeping place and a birthing chamber. There is no need for a large structure in which temperature regulation would be next to impossible.

• • •

Life in the Arctic is dependent on snow. It is the only source of fresh water when lakes and rivers freeze into solid ice. More importantly, its insulating properties are unsurpassed. A small fat-burning lamp can heat an igloo. A layer of snow 20 inches (50 cm) deep will keep the temperature at soil level near freezing even when the mercury drops to –40° above the surface. Entire communities of rodents depend on snow for survival. Newborn polar bear cubs would freeze to death without the protection of their den. Even when blizzards engulf the land, temperatures inside hover around the freezing point. And snow is 90 percent trapped air, enabling gas exchange between the interior of the den and the outside and preventing the animal from suffocating. As the walls of the den ice up, the female scrapes away the glaze, allowing carbon dioxide to escape and oxygen to filter in.

In most areas polar bear dens are dug into snowdrifts. The entrance tunnel is usually about 6.5 feet (2 m) long but very narrow, about 25 inches (65 cm) in diameter. The tunnel leads to a single chamber 6.5 by 5 feet (2 m by 1.5 m) in area and 3 feet (1 m) high, which is usually slightly higher than the entrance in order to trap warmer air. In northern Alaska, many females have abandoned their den sites on land because of increased disturbance in the wake of oil exploration and the development of ice roads along the coast. They have started constructing maternity dens in the lee of pressure ridges on the multiyear ice pack in the Beaufort Sea. However, the ice is an unstable medium and moves hundreds of miles over the course of the winter, so breeding success has been low.

In northern Manitoba and northern Ontario on the Hudson Bay coast, polar bear maternity dens lie within the limits of the forest. Because females enter the dens before there is sufficient snow cover in this southern locale, the den extends into the soil on the side of a small rise, its roof stabilized by the root systems of the trees above. While in most other areas the dens collapse over the summer, these survive and are sometimes used for generations. As the season progresses, a snowdrift forms over the entrance, keeping the den warm when the cubs are born.

Most grizzlies' dens are excavations of similar size as or slightly smaller than those of polar bears. They are dug into the slope of a hill or mountain. In the

The southern shore of Hudson Bay is the only place where the denning area of polar bears lies in the transitional zone between tundra and boreal forest. A female with her cubs rests among a cluster of trees on her week-long journey out to the sea ice, 40 miles (65 km) distant.

TOP: During adverse conditions polar bears often hunker down in the lee of a snowdrift until the weather improves. Covered by snow, they become all but invisible.

BOTTOM: The trek out to the sea ice is an arduous undertaking for the new cubs. The female frequently stops to nurse and rest her off-spring.

Far North, where the climate is colder but also drier, bears select den sites in locations where snow accumulates. In a study in the Northwest Territories, average snow depth above the den entrance was 30 inches (76 cm), even though just a short distance away the snow depth averaged 6 inches (15 cm). Only in temperate zones such as the West Coast of British Columbia can the animals afford to forsake the protection of an earth den and have their young in small caves or large rock crevices.

Black bears use a variety of den sites, from an excavation in the ground to a pit below a fallen log or a depression in a dense stand of saplings. They have even been known to use structures provided by humans, such as a culvert underneath a highway and even the basement of a house (the owner had no idea of the unusual cohabitant). Pregnant females select hollow trees when available, as they provide better insulation. A female expends 15 percent less energy during hibernation in a tree den than in a ground den, so average cub survival is better. However, because only trees over 150 years old are large

enough to contain hollows suitable for a bear to use, and because mature stands of hardwood trees are rare in many areas – a result of prevailing logging practices – tree dens are often not an option. Proper site selection is crucial for denning success. Over much of the black bear's range, weather conditions in the winter are extremely variable. In a sudden warm spell dens are subject to flooding. If this happens to a female with a new litter, she has no choice but to relocate to a different site. The survival rate for the cubs in such cases is only 40 percent.

Apart from providing protection from the environment, the den also has to serve as a safe refuge. The more vulnerable a bear, particularly if she's a female with cubs of the year, the more important this aspect becomes. Bears in hibernation have a limited ability to defend themselves, as they are in a confined area. They can't avoid an aggressor and are further handicapped by a reduced metabolic rate. Adult males sometimes dig into the dens of other bears and kill the occupants. Even wolves have been reported to penetrate black bear dens. It is quite possible that the large variety of den sites used by black bears today is a human artifact. Tree hollows have become scarce and the wolf and other large predators have been eliminated over much of their former range, so excavation dens are now a viable alternative.

· · ·

Soon curiosity wins out over fear and the three small polar bear cubs appear again in the mouth of the den. From their tender, helpless beginnings they have grown into rambunctious bundles of energy weighing 22 pounds (10 kg). The walls of the den have already experienced their exploratory enthusiasm. Over the past months they have dug small alcoves into the sides, extending the boundaries of their snowy underworld. But now that their mother has broken through the entrance to the den, a whole new realm has opened up. One by one they climb into the sunlight and approach their mother. Quickly all fear of this novel world evaporates as they scale her body and begin a game of king of the castle. One cub loses its balance and slides down the drift to the bottom. A new entertainment is discovered. Cubs know only two speeds: full throttle or a complete halt. Thirty minutes later they lie down exhausted next to their mother and fall asleep.

· · ·

Female polar bears stay with their cubs at the den for as long as two weeks after emerging. Although the days are already longer, temperatures are still frigid. The time spent around the den is time spent acclimatizing. At night she returns inside for warmth. For cubs this is a harsh environment; their dense coat is all that protects them from the cold. The fur consists of thick underwool and long, clear guard hair. Thirty years ago, aerial surveys of polar bear populations discovered that the animal shows up on ultraviolet-sensitive film. The bear's coat absorbs UV radiation, whereas the surrounding snow reflects it. Further investigation revealed that the clear guard hairs direct ultraviolet light to the animal's dark skin, helping it stay warm.

Adult animals probably benefit little from this unique adaptation. A layer of fat as much as 4 inches (11 cm) thick prevents that slight warming of the skin from penetrating to the core of the body. Also, in the dead of winter, when conditions are at their worst, there is no or very little sunlight over most of the animal's range. Thus, when an adult animal would benefit most from this adaptation, the least ultraviolet light is available. For cubs, however, the situation is quite different. By the time they follow their mother out onto the sea ice, the sun spends at least 11 hours above the horizon. And cubs need any thermal help they can get. For them the peculiar features of their coat may mean the difference between life and death.

After leaving the denning area, the female will still occasionally dig snow caves to provide shelter for her offspring on cold days. She has to be particularly careful about crossing leads, or openings in the ice. Young, growing and hence lean, her progeny can swim only short distances without getting hypothermic. Consequently females try to avoid open water with their new litters. And if a crossing can't be avoided, the family rests afterward to give the cubs a chance to nurse and warm up.

Waters conducts heat 20 times better than air. Although salt water cannot cool below 25°F (–4°C) before turning to ice, without protection the core temperature of a submerged mammal in such conditions quickly drops to a point where the animal loses consciousness. To avoid hypothermia, most marine mammals such as seals and whales are covered in a layer of blubber. Others, such as the sea otter, rely entirely on their coat for protection. The denser the fur, the better the insulation, as the individual fibers trap air. On a sea otter 100,000 individual strands of hair crowd each square centimeter. The winter coat of a polar bear is by comparison a flimsy affair. As only 1,500 hairs share a square centimeter, the animal gets soaked to the skin when it dives into the frigid sea. Adult bears rely on their layer of fat to keep them warm, a protection unavailable to cubs. The polar bear's coat is much better suited to providing an insulating layer on land, but the hair does display an adaptation to the aquatic lifestyle. If a brown or black bear gets wet on a frosty day, ice forms in its coat. Polar bears don't have that problem because their oily fur sheds water quickly. To assist the natural qualities of their coat, the animals also roll in the snow to get rid of any excess moisture.

The Arctic fox is a frequent companion of the polar bear. *Nanook,* the great bear, provides them with food sources as they eke out a living scavenging leftovers. Individual foxes become quite defensive of their bear and chase off approaching competitors.

. . .

Two weeks later the female show signs of restlessness. A blizzard has kept the family inside for three days. As the morning finally dawns calm, she decides to leave the familiar surroundings of the den and strike out for the sea ice. For the past eight months she has been fasting, since the last of the pack ice melted in the previous July. At first she rested on the coast for a while. Then, as the weather cooled in September, she moved inland to find a den site. Now, at the end of March, her fat deposits have shrunk. She needs to hunt to replenish her bodily reserves. Out on Hudson Bay the ringed seals, her main prey, will soon have their young. The best time of the year for the polar bear is approaching – a time of gluttony, when the animals feed on pups and inexperienced juvenile seals.

In the past few weeks her cubs have added a few more pounds to their frame. They have also got used to the weather conditions; now they appear impervious to the cold. The female leads her cubs unwaveringly northeast. The way to the best hunting grounds is long and strenuous. Sixty miles (100 km) of pathless terrain lie ahead of the family. From the outset the cubs struggle in the deep snow among the trees. When the procession grinds to a halt in a deep drift of powder, she ferries them across on her back until she reaches packed ground again. At the end of the day, having covered but 5 miles (8 km), she comes across the unoccupied den of another family and settles in for the night.

Three days later the polar bear female and her cubs reach the convoluted landscape of the sea ice. Instead of soft snow it is now pressure ridges that slow their advance. Time and again the female lifts her cubs over obstacles. But slowly the smallest of her young – the runt – begins to show signs of exhaustion. He starts to lag behind, and collapses as soon as the family stops to rest. The physical exercise has increased the cubs' appetite, and the littermates now compete more aggressively for nursing privileges. As the days pass the small cub weakens visibly. His mother patiently waits for him to catch up and occasionally even walks back to softly encourage him to follow. However, as female bears don't intervene in the fights and arguments of their young, the runt, the weakest, loses out every time the cubs drink.

In the waning days of March a blizzard blows up out of the north and temperatures drop rapidly. In the lee of a pressure ridge the female digs a small cave into which the family retreats. At some point during the night the cold penetrates the runt's fur and enters into him. Even for the supreme predator of the Arctic wilderness it is a hard life, and only rarely are mother polar bears able to raise three cubs.

April

Chapter Three

An Exciting World

It is late April. Serrated rocky crests tower ominously above a valley clothed in a dark mantle of mature pine and fir. The mountains seem to pierce the sky. Snow still lies heavy in the high country. Only down near the rushing river has winter lost its grip on the land. In the shade of the trees a few dirty patches of slush linger, but the warming sun has freed the meadows. A grizzly, trailed by two small cubs, digs for the roots of sweet vetch and the bulbs of glacier lilies at the edge of the water. In the four months since their birth the youngsters have developed into boisterous small bears weighing about 12 pounds (5–6 kg). The female has been busy this morning – half of the forest clearing looks as if it has been freshly rototilled. A clump of dirt flies backward from between her legs and hits one of the cubs in the head. A surprised yelp escapes the youngster's mouth. It jumps aside, but then returns to investigate the projectile. Everything the female touches is thoroughly inspected with eyes, nose and mouth. Young bears learn what is edible from watching and copying their mother. Cubs orphaned at an early age prefer only a limited range of food sources, whereas bears that stay longer with their mother enjoy a much broader spectrum of mountain cuisine.

The attention span of the cub is short. When the pile of sod shows no intention of moving, even after much prodding, something or someone else has to serve as a play partner. And siblings are usually open to any diversion offered. At present the cub's brother is deeply involved in chewing a branch into submission. But a short pull on the stick shifts his interest. Within seconds the cubs are embroiled in a wrestling match. With obvious delight they throw punches and bite each other's neck and shoulders.

The peacefulness of the morning comes to an abrupt end – near the edge of the forest, only 50 yards (46 m) away, a twig breaks with a sharp snap. The female is immediately alarmed. Her head shoots up and she stares nervously into the darkness beneath the trees. She pops her jaws to call her offspring to her side. There is no hesitation on their part, no questioning her signal; they obey immediately. The playfulness they displayed just seconds before is replaced by agitation and fear. They race over to her and push their bodies against hers. Then they stand up, their front paws resting on her side, and scrutinize the woods in front of them. Among the shadows of the trees the dark contour of a large animal is vaguely discernable. For a few seconds the adult male bear hesitates, then steps into the light. As he enters the meadow the female whirls around and races off toward the opposite side, her young trailing but a couple of yards behind.

The cubs are her first litter. She herself has just grown into adulthood, and barely so. Female brown bears, like polar bears, reach sexual maturity at the age of five, males at the age of seven. Black bears develop a little faster, generally a year ahead of their bigger cousins. However, these are average values, and some bears reach sexual maturity earlier. The first attempt at raising cubs is not usually crowned with success, as the female is inexperienced and still hasn't reached her full size. The physical demands of motherhood often prove too much of a strain.

It was inexperience that led the female to select her den site. The soil didn't drain well and her den was exposed to the south. Though it was high up on the mountain, when spring started early she was forced out of their domicile with her cubs by melt water running into it. Early in the season, females with cubs of the year usually remain in the high country. Food is not more plentiful there – on the contrary. But the lower elevations are occupied by other bears foraging for scarce resources. Families stay up high to avoid members of their own species. The young female would have kept away from the valley floor as well, if the deep snow cover on the upper slopes hadn't rendered her foraging endeavors fruitless.

Two grizzly cubs curiously inspect their surroundings while their mother grazes on new shoots. Early in the season, mountain grizzlies feed heavily on grasses and roots.

· · ·

TOP: In contrast to the golden eagle, bald eagles have not been observed killing cubs. However, they have been seen feeding on bear carcasses.

BOTTOM: Recent evidence suggests that cub mortality caused by wolves is much higher than previously assumed.

Spring is the hardest time of the year for both grizzlies and black bears. It's a time of acute food shortage. After the long sleep, many bears are in dire need of replenishing spent fat deposits. Most bears that succumb to starvation don't die in their den in the dead of winter. They are forced to vacate their cold-season retreat early and prowl the mountains, increasingly desperate. It is a gamble they have no choice but to take, and it is their life that is at stake. The animals look for carrion – bighorn sheep that died in an avalanche or mule deer that lost the battle with the cold. Often other scavengers such as wolves, wolverines and ravens have already cleaned everything up. But, particularly in avalanche chutes, those competitors are often not able to penetrate the compacted ice to get to the carcasses, which become the bear's spoils.

In spring the mountains are a hungry land, and it is a dangerous time for cubs of the year. One-third of the young never live to see their first birthday and 60 percent never grow to adulthood. Some die of diseases, others starve to death. And some get killed. Although we see bears as lords of the forest, mountains and tundra, they are not invulnerable. Wolves follow polar bear females with new litters in an apparent attempt to separate a young one from its mother. While never confirmed for polar bears, successful hunts by wolves on grizzly cubs have been witnessed. Even golden eagles will occasionally swoop down and snatch a cub early in the season. In the forests, mountain lions, lynx and bobcats pose a threat. But it is other bears the females have to worry about most.

Bears are opportunistic by nature. With the exception of a female with her cubs, they don't live in permanent social units. The animals compete over resources. Consequently, interactions between individuals are antagonistic at first. Bears may engage in play with one other, but only after appeasement behavior to confirm good intentions. The animals are always a potential threat to another of their species, particularly if there is a large difference in size. For grizzlies and black bears this is especially true in early spring, when food is an all-consuming obsession. With few resources available, the animals are much more inclined to turn to cannibalistic behavior to get a meal. Consequently most females with a new litter steer clear of all other bears for the first couple of months after emerging from the den.

In contrast to grizzlies and black bears, spring is a time of plenty for the polar bear. Yet even polar bear females shun the hunting grounds of large males when the cubs are still small. While the males may show little interest in the cubs and are more tolerant of other bears when food is abundant, chance encounters can occur. Cubs just a few months old are defenseless. They cannot outrun a larger bear. And out on the ice there are no trees to climb to safety.

Infanticide, the killing of the young of one's own species, has been observed in bears on numerous occasions. Some consider it the main cause of mortality in cubs, though this is hard to prove in the wild, as the death of a young one most often goes unwitnessed. Originally infanticide confused biologists and was seen as aberrant behavior, the action of a bear with – to put it in human terms – psychotic tendencies. But in the 1970s two scientists, Sarah Hrdy and Glenn Hausfater, proposed that infanticidal behavior can under certain circumstances increase the reproductive success of the perpetrator. The competition's progeny is eliminated, and many a time a female will go into estrus, or readiness to mate, again within a few weeks of losing her young, giving the male an opportunity to pass on his own genetic material. This theory has been proven correct for a number of species, including many rodents and some primates. The most well-known example is lions, but even there the issue of infanticidal behavior as a reproductive strategy isn't clear-cut. In

A brown bear cub feeds on the remains of a yearling killed in a confrontation between the mothers. Contrary to common belief, the perpetrators of infanticide are not always adult males – frequently they are females.

A large male polar bear on the Hudson Bay coast consumes a juvenile he has killed. Bears, probably like all predators, are opportunistic cannibals, particularly when food is scarce.

55

A grizzly cub explores its environment under the watchful eye of its mother. For a young bear, playful investigation of its surroundings is an integral part of growing up.

some populations infanticide is practiced by the males, in others not. It appears to occur only in populations of lions that are non-seasonal breeders, meaning that the lioness may come into estrus at any time of the year.

Some bear biologists greeted this new theory enthusiastically. It offered an explanation that gave evolutionary meaning to a confusing aspect of bear behavior. Incidents of infanticide committed by male bears were uncritically explained as an attempt by an animal to increase its chances of reproducing. However, as more information became available, this line of thought was questioned. For one thing, bears are seasonal breeders, yet cubs get killed long after the breeding season, when the female cannot go into estrus again after losing her cubs. In all species in which infanticide as a reproductive strategy has been observed, parental males protect their offspring. Male bears, on the other hand, don't get involved with the raising of cubs in any way. Also, for the female to come into estrus she has to lose her entire litter. Only in one instance was a bear observed to kill an entire litter, and in that case it was another female that committed the infanticide. Furthermore, as the female does not become sexually receptive until a number of weeks after losing her litter, there is no direct feedback, and any one of a number of males could reap the sexual benefits of the situation.

Victims of intraspecies killings are not restricted to one age class. Females die while defending cubs. Juveniles fall victim to other bears. And none of these cases help a male to reproduce. While large males are often the aggressors in these murderous activities, females are involved as well. It appears scientifically questionable to select, out of all cases of infanticide and intraspecies killings, only those that might match a theory – or at least not contradict it – while ignoring the rest. Most likely all such cases have their roots in the opportunistic feeding habits and the social structure of a bear population. It has even been suggested that infanticide is a mode of population control.

. . .

The young female does not care about the motives of a potentially infanticidal bear. Her concern is the safety of her cubs, and she is not interested in finding out whether the male has any interest in her or her offspring. At the far end of the meadow she turns around and stands up.

. . .

Contrary to common belief, vision in bears is about comparable to a human's. They are not shortsighted, as often stated, and they can also see colors. The confusion over the accuracy of their vision stems from observations that a bear very often trusts its nose rather than its eyes when identifying an unknown object. This is a testament to the quality of bears' olfactory sense rather than proof of deficiency in their vision. A bear's sense of smell is approximately as acute as a dog's. By comparison, our ability to detect odor is almost nonexistent. We are very much focused and dependent on visual perception, and this is probably why we have so much difficulty comprehending that any animal would rather rely on the nose than the eyes.

For a bear, as Kenneth Grahame put it, scents are fairy calls from the void. Odors are messengers. A male polar bear was observed to walk in a straight line for 30 miles (50 km) to a female in estrus – his nose picked up her scent. The animals can detect the lair of a seal from over half a mile away, even if it's covered by 3 feet (1 m) of snow. They are able to locate breathing holes from a distance of 1,300 feet (400 m). The noses of grizzlies and black bears are probably just as good. And, while unable to hold a candle to bears' sense of smell, their hearing is good as well. They may, like dogs, be able to hear sounds beyond the range of human ears. This has not been scientifically verified, however.

. . .

Without displaying much interest, the large male watches the female run off. He walks over to where she has dug up the ground, sniffs her tracks, glances once again in her direction and then starts feeding. Satisfied that he is not pursuing her and her family, the female lowers herself back on all fours and moves off through the trees. The meadow is now the male's by right of his larger size. In a bear's world, bigger is definitely better – the right of first possession is seldom enforceable.

A female brown bear and her cub attentively watch a large male nearby before turning away and avoiding the potential threat.

May

Chapter Four

The Mating Game

Behind a curtain of rain the mountains on the far side of the bay are only vaguely visible, as if being born from a hazy memory. In spring, as the land warms and the oceans remain cool, the usual flow of air is reversed. The meteorological high over central Alaska is pushed inland and giant low-pressure systems move north along the Aleutian chain. As a consequence, rain and wind are part of life on the Alaska Peninsula. But this is also a land of change. Half an hour later the deluge ends as suddenly as it started. Deep blue patches of sky are lost behind windswept shreds of clouds. Occasionally the afternoon sun finds a hole and beams its spotlight on the vast sedge flats below.

Early in the year, during the sedges' growing season and before they go into bloom, the tips of these grasses contain as much as 25 percent protein. From late May until mid-July brown bears feed heavily on them. As many as 70 animals share a bay 5 miles (8 km) wide. During the downpour only a single bear, a large male, was feeding out in the open, unperturbed by the rain. Now, as the shower ceases, more animals leave the cover of the cottonwood trees and join him. Soon 10 grizzlies are spread out across the flats grazing on the sedge, reminiscent more of buffalo than the popular image of the unpredictable, moody ruler of the North American wilderness.

Next to a tidal creek draining the sedge flats a blond female shears off the tops of the grass blades with her teeth. She doesn't even lift her head to chew and swallow. Only 50 feet (15 m) behind her feeds a large male, his muzzle and shoulder heavily scarred. He is huge by comparison, easily weighing twice as much as the female.

• • •

A male brown bear on the Alaska coast weighs over 1,000 pounds (450 kg). Exceptional individuals may tip the scales at 1,500 pounds (700 kg), though such monsters are rare. Male polar bears reach a similar size, the largest individuals being slightly heavier than their brown bear counterparts. They are the largest terrestrial carnivores. Grizzlies in the interior don't grow to such extremes; a very large male may weigh in at 770 pounds (350 kg). Male black bears are considerably smaller, on average weighing about 300 pounds (130 kg). However, exceptional males of much larger size have been found. In early September 2001, a black bear was hit by a car northeast of Winnipeg, Manitoba. The animal was huge, weighing over 900 pounds (400 kg).

Females are always much smaller than their male counterparts. This difference in size is referred to as sexual dimorphism. In bears, the larger the species, the more pronounced the sexual dimorphism. The tropical sun bear, the smallest of all bears, shows the smallest size difference between the sexes. A large male polar bear, on the other hand, is over twice as heavy as a female. The same holds true for the giants among the grizzlies.

Fierce competition for breeding rights is seen as the reason for pronounced sexual dimorphism in bears. The bear population is roughly evenly divided into males and females. However, females accompanied by cubs are not available as mates during the breeding season. The result is that several males must compete for the favors of one female. As larger individuals have an advantage in defending breeding rights, and hence greater success in passing on their genetic material to the next generation than smaller ones, during the course of evolution the males became bigger. But the impact of an increase in size is more profound than what meets the eye. A larger animal needs more food; thus the home ranges of males are bigger than those of females. This also increases the likelihood of finding a receptive mating partner, as a male's home range will overlap the home ranges of several females.

The mating season for polar bears starts in April and extends into June. Brown bears mate later, between May and July. Most black bears don't

LEFT: **Most female grizzlies reach sexual maturity at the age of five. Often their first attempts at raising young fail due to inexperience.**

RIGHT: **At half the size of a full-grown adult, this juvenile male polar bear will be unable to compete for mating privileges for several more years.**

engage in amorous activities until June. Although the mating season of bears covers several months, females are in estrus for about three weeks only. And they will allow a male to mount them during just three to four days at the peak of the estrus cycle. As the animals for the most part lead a solitary existence, congregating in small areas only when food is abundant, they face a problem in finding a potential mate at the right time. Hence bears, dominant males in particular, travel far across their home ranges during the breeding season. Similar actions have been observed in females.

To detect a female in heat, bears primarily trust their noses. Metabolites of sex hormones are eliminated from the body with the urine. With their exceptionally acute sense of smell, males are able to determine the receptiveness of the female by sniffing the areas where she has urinated, walked or slept. Keeping their noses close to the ground, they will follow a promising scent trail unwaveringly for miles.

. . .

The blond female grazing next to the river moves to a new spot of sedges 300 feet (90 m) away. Her every step is mirrored by the large male. Several times he stops to sniff the ground where she has just walked. There is purpose to his movements, but also patience. She, on the other hand, seems nervous about his continued interest. Being larger is a knife that cuts both ways. While he is more able to ward off other suitors, she tries to evade the male because he is potentially dangerous to her.

For the next four days the unequal pair can be seen crossing meadows, ambling through brush and traveling along streams, always an unvarying

A female brown bear endures her male suitor. Acts of copulation may last as long as 45 minutes. As bears are thought to be induced ovulators, short copulation times may be insufficient to cause release of an ovum.

distance apart. Finally the female allows the male to come closer, and soon the animals are grazing, playing and resting in close proximity. After several days of this intimate togetherness, the female at last permits her suitor to mount. They copulate for 45 minutes. Afterward the animals rest, feed for a short while, and then copulate again.

. . .

Many questions about the mating of bears are still unsolved. In some populations with a low density of bears, males often try to sequester estrous females in valleys, by fjords or on mountaintops, away from other males, in order to protect breeding rights. In coastal ecosystems, where as many as 40 bears – including several estrous females and numerous adult males – may share a sedge flat during the breeding period, attempts to isolate the female are nowhere near as pronounced. While males try to restrict the movements of a female, they are unable to isolate her from competing males, and don't appear to attempt to do so. Often a breeding pair will walk by another adult male without even eliciting a reaction.

One hypothesis suggests that the dominant animals know exactly when the female has reached the peak of her estrus cycle, so they don't bother to compete until the decisive moment. But on numerous occasions a dominant male has been observed copulating with a female within 300 feet (90 m) of several potential competitors, without any of them showing interest in the matter. It is possible that the other males conceded to a bigger, stronger individual. But on a number of occasions the situation was reversed; a male that had been just an uninterested spectator became the suitor of another

A dominant male rises up on his hind legs in an attempt to impress and drive off another male competing for the same female.

Displaying his dominance, a large male rubs his back on alders, urinating at the same time, after winning a fight.

estrous female, while the male that had been copulating previously reverted to being a spectator.

At times competition is fierce. Males get injured in confrontations over the right to mate. Gaping lacerations on head, shoulders and front legs, as well as broken jaws and broken canine teeth, attest to the seriousness with which the battles are fought. But under what circumstances do these fights erupt, and why not always? In areas where bears congregate and breeding opportunities arise more frequently, possibly competition for mating rights is diminished and right of first possession comes into play.

Another factor may be the availability of food. The animals' general disposition toward members of their own species may be less antagonistic in areas with abundant resources. The animals are simply less stressed in the absence of intense competition for sustenance. Much of our knowledge of bear behavior has been collected in marginal habitats in which survival of the fittest requires a higher level of aggression. In most regions bears have been eradicated from the prime feeding areas. The remnant populations we investigate today may be providing us with information about the behavioral patterns of animals on the edge. What we consider to be the norm today may not have been standard behavior originally.

· · ·

While the blond female feeds, her large friend lies down a few yards away. Although he is resting amid a rich food source, he rarely grazes on the sedges, being more interested in protecting his interests. When other bears approach, it usually suffices for him to rise and walk a few steps in their direction to scatter them. Some young males hang around on the perimeter, just far enough away to be ignored by the large bear, yet still close enough to sneak in should his attention slacken. And at times he does get distracted. Beyond the female, another large male approaches. He is not as heavy as the first, but taller in the shoulder.

When the new arrival is still 450 feet (140 m) away, the scarred male rises to his feet. Then he stands up on his hind legs. With his front paws he pulls at invisible branches over his head and rubs his back against a nonexistent tree, urinating at the same time. Then he falls back on all fours and, in slow motion with his head held low, he walks toward the competitor. His hind legs and hips move in an overemphasized swagger often referred to as the cowboy walk.

His challenger is not easily impressed. They circle each other 100 feet (30 m) apart. Then both move over to a group of stunted spruce and repeat the rubbing action, this time leaving their scent and some hair on real bark, not air. Several trees receive their attentions. Repeated use over the years has polished the spruce trunks smooth. Numerous such "bear trees" line the sedge meadow. Their function is mostly to serve as signposts indicating an animal's presence to any other bear passing by. They are also used to establish

dominance, as the largest animal's mark will be the highest up the tree.

For almost 30 minutes the two males follow each other through the brush, periodically rubbing their backs on trees. There is never any physical contact, no roaring or fighting. The entire interaction consists of posturing, while apparently failing to convince the opponent. These displays of dominance seem almost to have taken on a meaning of their own – the female has meanwhile moved 1,300 feet (400 m) away. The males are too involved with each other to even notice.

A juvenile bear quickly walks over to the female. As he is only marginally larger than she is, she shows no fear. They touch noses. Then the young male moves around behind her and mounts. For 30 minutes they copulate, uninterrupted until the scarred male finally drives off his adult competition and takes the juvenile's place.

· · ·

Three siblings feed on sedges in southwestern Alaska. Littermates often remain together for one to two seasons after they are released into independence by their mother.

It is thought that the largest male fathers most of the cubs in a population. For a long time the same idea was postulated for ungulates (hoofed mammals), until it was discovered that subordinate males did most of the mating while the dominant animals were busy defending their harem. The same may be true for bears in some populations. However, without genetic testing this is impossible to prove, as the act of copulation does not necessarily result in fertilization of an ovum. Short copulation will most often not produce any offspring at all, as bears are thought to be induced ovulators.

Ovulation in mammals either occurs spontaneously (without any external trigger), as in humans, or is induced by the male, as in bears. Spontaneous ovulation harbors a risk that the ovum will die before conception is achieved. But for animals living in herds or family groups, the chance is small that no breeding partner will be encountered at the time of ovulation or soon after. Most bears, on the other hand, spend much of their adult life in voluntary separation from their fellow beasts. To guarantee

Three brown bear cubs of the year watch their mother fishing for salmon from the stream's edge. With many bears nearby, the cubs are fidgety, nervous and easily spooked.

that a fertile egg will be available at the time of copulation, ovulation happens only with appropriate mechanical stimulation. Characteristic of mammals that are induced ovulators are a long copulation time and a so-called penis bone, or baculum. In a large male brown bear the baculum is slightly longer than a pen and twice as thick. How long copulation must last to trigger ovulation is a question that has still not been answered.

Litters of bear cubs are fraternal rather than identical multiple births. Because each ovulation produces but one ovum, several copulations are required to stimulate the release of the eggs and fertilize them. Particularly in an area where bears occur in high concentrations during the mating season, females will sometimes mate with several males. This situation arises primarily when a subordinate individual is chased off by a dominant animal. Females possibly even select numerous partners as a strategy to discourage infanticide. Whatever the reason, the cubs of one litter can all have different fathers.

. . .

For another two days the uneven pair remains bonded. Then the female loses interest in such close contact, appears to grow uncomfortable in the proximity of the male, and wanders off. The male uses his regained independence to search for further prospective mates. His involvement in the future generation has come to an end. From now on it will be solely the female's duty to raise the young, protect them from danger and introduce them to the secrets of a bear's life.

Seeking comfort in physical contact, two brown bear cubs cuddle up to their mother as they watch another bear nearby. Cream-colored cubs are rare. Their coats will darken to a silver gray as they grow older.

June

Chapter Five

The Fight for Survival

Under the midnight sun just north of the Arctic Circle, channels of water have developed on the pack ice out in Foxe Basin, an arm of the sea that separates Baffin Island from the Canadian mainland. Nature in the Far North paints in few colors – the latticework of cobalt channels is draped like a fishnet over a vast expanse of white. The ice-covered surface of the ocean has been transformed into an Arctic Venice of shallow canals only one to two feet (30–60 cm) deep. A female polar bear with two yearling cubs moves across her ever-changing domain with a steady lumbering gait, sometimes following the blue channels, occasionally traversing them.

The mother guides her family northwest. In contrast to terrestrial bears, her home changes over the seasons, from week to week, and even on a daily basis. Winds and currents open leads and close them again. Ice forms, then melts. In many places there are no landmarks to navigate by. Yet the animals travel with great precision. Season after season they unerringly return to the same hunting grounds.

. . .

Radio-collared bears have been tracked to within a few miles of the location they were found at the previous year, an astonishing feat considering that ice is a continuously moving platform. How bears navigate is not known. Their ability to follow a compass bearing has many a time astounded researchers and bear managers. Relocation of problem bears, for instance, is more often than not ineffective. Both black bears and grizzlies frequently return to their home range in a direct line through hundreds of miles of unknown territory.

A brown bear that was moved from the coastal town of Cordova in Alaska to the opposite side of Prince William Sound was spotted back in his former haunts within two weeks. On his return trip the animal had swum across a busy shipping lane and several ocean channels over 6 miles (10 km) wide, with strong tidal currents. When released, relocated black bears in a study immediately headed in the direction of their place of origin. Their movements became random only when the animals had been transported over 600 miles (1,000 km). Because the bears followed a compass heading regardless of cloud cover and time of day of release, some scientists feel that the animals may use the earth's magnetic field for navigation, much as some migratory birds do.

Polar bears often appear misleadingly casual and inattentive to their surroundings as they plod across the ice, the large head swinging from side to side as they walk. But little passes unnoticed. Their entire existence is a fusion of two life principles: the need for energy conservation and the provision of sufficient nourishment. There is nothing laid-back about these animals. Even their deceivingly slow but steady gait averages about 3.5 miles (5.5 km) per hour over uneven terrain, a brisk walking speed for a human on level ground.

. . .

Every little while the female stops, scans the surrounding area and continues on her way. Her cubs sometimes trail behind to investigate a crack in the ice or an old track, then break into a run to catch up with their mother. All of a sudden the female freezes in her tracks as if she has walked into an invisible wall. The cubs are caught off guard and stumble into her rear end. They regain their composure quickly and look curiously around her to discover the reason for her change in attitude. A thousand feet (300 m) away the dark outline of a ringed seal sprawls on the ice. Every 30 seconds the animal lifts its head to check for danger and then plops down again for another quick power nap. Seals never haul out next to a breathing hole in groups, as they would interfere with each other's getaway trying to squeeze through the same escape hatch. Thus they do not benefit from the cumulative awareness of a multitude of eyes. Every animal depends on itself to detect a predator. Sleep is a luxury seals cannot afford.

The female studies the surface of the ice for several minutes, looking for

Pulling off the seal's skin, the polar bear exposes the thick layer of blubber underneath. Adult bears often devour just the fat and leave the muscle tissue behind, which is then scavenged by juvenile bears, Arctic foxes and ravens.

ABOVE: **In many areas the only feasible way to monitor habitat use is with radio collars. In adult male polar bears the neck is wider than the head, and thus they defy traditional methods of attaching transmitters. Miniaturization now makes them small enough to be glued to the skin.**

FACING PAGE: **Curiosity and hunger often bring young, inexperienced bears into conflict with man.**

a possible route to the intended dinner, evaluating different approaches. Then she makes up her mind. With a short, rough *huff* she orders her cubs to stay put and out of sight. Carefully she lowers her body into the shallow canal in front of her. Not even a ripple betrays her presence. Lying flat on her belly, she will be able to remain invisible to the seal until she is right on him. Her nose and eyes barely break the surface as she slides along quietly, propelling herself with her paws extended to the sides to keep as low a profile as possible. About halfway to her quarry the channel forks. For a moment the female stops, then continues on in the wrong channel, away from her prey. Only a few yards later she realizes her mistake and backtracks without lifting her head – an amazing demonstration of the power of recollection in bears and their ability to develop and execute strategy.

Lying motionless for any length of time is a hard lesson for a young bear to learn. Patience is a virtue that is attained through age, and it's in short supply with the youngsters. One of the cubs is getting bored and bites his sibling playfully on the shoulder. Lacking an enthusiastic response from his brother, he rises up to check on his mother's progress. But even after scanning in every direction, he is unable to locate her. Sniffing the ice where she slipped into the channel, he slowly starts to follow the ribbon of water. The yearling hasn't got very far when the seal notices the movement. With a loud splash it dives into the ocean.

Just yards from the breathing hole, the female rises to her feet. Her posture radiates frustration. The seal never knew how close it was to death. After inspecting the entrance to the water world below, the female turns around. There is no point in waiting; the seal will not return after being spooked. The animals always keep several holes open and readily abandon one that has been proven unsafe.

As the female notices her cub and realizes the reason for the hunt's failure, her anger boils over. She cuffs the youngster hard, growling loudly. The yearling rolls over on his side, crying submissively. Scared by the commotion, the second cub peeks nervously over the rim of the ice ridge he has been hiding behind. In an effort to appease his mother, the first cub, his head held low, gently licks the corner of her mouth. The female is quickly mollified. The yearling still has much to learn. Next spring at the start of the mating season she will sever the apron strings, and the cubs will be left to their own devices. Their survival will depend on their ability to secure food by themselves.

• • •

The first year of independence is the hardest. As many as one-third of juveniles do not reach sexual maturity. Starvation is the reason, and it is starving juveniles that cause most of the trouble with people. Still, accidents are rare. Although polar bears have a reputation for being the only bears that stalk humans as prey, the fact is that a healthy adult animal will

avoid people. If polar bears were generally intent on killing people, either there would be no Inuit living in the Arctic or the beast would have been eradicated – there can be no coexistence with a man-killer. The problem is that polar bears range over vast areas, and one never knows when a starving animal might be close by.

Often siblings stay together for as long as a couple of years. In areas of high concentration of brown bears it has been observed that juveniles from several litters will form small gangs and prowl the region in one another's company. Occasionally they even harass other bears. Safety lies in numbers. Two may be able to defend a carcass where one would lose it to a larger or simply more confident individual. However, that is where the cooperation ends.

A bear's prey is too small to warrant collaborative hunting, so for an adult animal there is nothing to gain from working together – the price of sharing the food is higher than the reward. Thus all adult bears, regardless of species, do not live in fixed social units. The only exceptions are females caring for young. Even in congregations such as along a salmon stream or at a beached whale, each adult bear acts independently, as an individual. In family units also the members don't cooperate in the hunt. The cubs watch, stalk separately and mostly interfere with the actions of the female. If she catches her quarry, it is despite the intervention of her offspring, not because of it.

Because environmental conditions and resource availability vary greatly

A female with her cub tests the sturdiness of a sheet of ice. For polar bears a successful hunt often depends on accurately judging the thickness of a layer of ice or snow in order to be able to break through with a single pounce, preventing their prey from escaping.

A juvenile brown bear being pursued by its mother races to safety. Many young attempt to rejoin their mother for some time after family ties are severed, and are frequently met with a violent response.

over the distribution range of bear species in North America, there is considerable variability in the age at which cubs are weaned. In resource-rich areas, litters on average are larger and the young bears are released sooner into independence. The time frame of parental guidance depends largely on the growth rate of the cubs. Young bears have to reach a certain size to stand a fair chance of making it on their own. For black bears over much of their southern temperate range, cubs are usually weaned at one and a half years. In southern Hudson Bay, 40 percent of polar bear females regard their parental duties complete when the young are that age. However, over much of a polar bear's and most of the brown bear's range, cubs are kept for two and a half years. About 15 percent of the females keep their progeny for a third year. And occasionally some fortunate cubs remain for four years under the protective maternal wing.

The separation of the family can come as a gradual drifting apart. But often the female, to the consternation of her offspring, quite suddenly quits tolerating her progeny and chases them off violently. The episode can be traumatic to the young, particularly if it is a single cub. The female is frequently observed soon after in the company of a male, so it is assumed that hormonal change lies behind her aggressive behavior toward her offspring that leads to the severance of family ties.

Occasionally very small bears are spotted on their own – smaller than they should be to tackle life independently from their mother. Although mortality among adult bears is low at 5 percent, females sometimes get killed or mortally injured in confrontations with other bears or in accidents, or they are shot. An orphan's chances of survival depend on age, species and luck. Polar bear cubs are the least likely to survive on their own, as their food source is wary prey, and hunting success relies on the experience and size of the hunter. Yearling brown bears stand a better chance because they feed to a large extent on vegetable matter. They may not be able to forage in the best habitat, but often they can secure enough to pull through. There is no record of orphaned grizzly cubs of the year surviving through their first winter in the wild. Winters in the remaining grizzly habitat are too long and cold, and cubs of the year have insufficient fat deposits to hibernate for several months on their own. However, young black bears that lose their mother at eight months can make it if conditions are optimal, that is, a good fall crop followed by a mild winter.

A romantic notion prevails that strange females will adopt orphans. However, this has been observed in the wild only very rarely. In one case a grizzly with two yearlings accepted an orphan into her family after the cub's mother vanished. The adopting female may have been the grandmother of the youngster. Though such adoptions are the exception, attempts of bereaved cubs to join families have been repeatedly observed. The orphans probably look for safety in the presence of other bears and other cubs, which because of their similar size are the only members of their species they are not afraid of. In human societies the adoption of orphans is an expression of compassion and graciousness. But a bear is not human, so different rules apply. When we adopt an orphan we don't risk the survival of our own children – our social structure is different. A female bear that adopts the offspring of another bear decreases the survival chances of her own cubs. Resources have to be shared with another mouth; the average weight of cubs decreases as litter size increases; and protection of a larger litter is also more difficult.

The persistence of the belief that bears will adopt orphans is based in part on the fact that occasionally family units have been observed in which litter members have different mothers. However, such mixed litters are most likely the result of a phenomenon called cub-swapping, which is caused by confusion over cub identity. Animals that raise their offspring in relative isolation often display a limited ability to identify their own progeny. This is also true in reverse, meaning that the ability of the young to recognize their mother is no better.

Cases of cub-swapping have been observed repeatedly along salmon streams. Primarily this happens when several family groups with young of equal age fish the same part of the river, and the cubs mingle. With so many bears around, the cubs are agitated, nervous and all too ready to leave the river with the first departing female. In some instances females have been seen arriving at the river with a litter of three and leaving with ten. Mostly the young bears are reunited with their biological mother within a few hours. Occasionally, however, they remain permanently with the foster family. In general the foster mother appears to have little problem with the new addition to her family as long as the strange cub stays calm. Should the adopted bear become nervous, bellowing in fear for its true mother, acceptance by the foster parent may turn into lethal intolerance.

It seems odd that identification of their own offspring should be difficult for bears, especially considering their excellent noses. But the issue isn't as clear-cut as one would think. A black bear female, for instance, will adopt a strange cub while she is still in the maternity den. After den emergence, however, the same female will kill any strange young. Scientists believe this results from an impeded sense of smell while in hibernation. Brown bear females that got separated from their young were able to identify and follow the scent track of their cubs, so recognition is possible. It may be that cub-swapping is caused by mixing of the odor of cubs of different litters as they play with and touch each other, which is then furthered by the females' preference to err on the safe side rather than reject or kill their own in a high-stress situation. Observing bears for a long time causes one truth to emerge clearly: there are no absolutes in the realm of animal behavior.

July

Chapter Six

Tales of Summer

At the base of a white pine a black bear nurses her two offspring. The female sits in repose, her back resting against the rough trunk of the mature tree. The cubs have placed themselves on either side of her, half standing on their hind legs, half lying on top of her, suckling on her nipples. Their contented humming is audible from 160 feet (50 m) away. As the milk flow slackens they change teats, only to return for a second try as soon as the flow ebbs at the new source.

. . .

Black bears, like grizzlies, have six nipples, four on the chest and two in the groin. Although rudimentary nipples are also found on the abdomen, the mammary glands there are inactive. When the female is curled up in the den, they would be hidden in a fold of her body and inaccessible to her young. Polar bear females, which have the richest milk, have but four teats, on their chest. This is seen as an evolutionary response to a smaller number of cubs.

Most polar bear females have two offspring. Triplets are rare, and quadruplets almost unheard of. In grizzlies and black bears triplets are the norm – the average litter contains 2.7 cubs. In some areas, such as Kodiak Island, a female parading along the salmon streams with a set of quadruplets is spotted in most years. The record number of cubs in a litter is six. However, such a large family is about as rare as naturally conceived quintuplets in humans, and survival chances are minimal for most of the young in such a large litter.

Nursing sessions usually last from six to eight minutes when the cubs are still small. As the young bears grow older, stronger and more efficient at suckling, they drink for only three to four minutes. Cubs continue to nurse until they are weaned, although during their first summer they are already supplementing their diet with grasses, roots, herbs and anything else the female feeds on.

Commonly the hormones associated with lactation inhibit the menstrual cycle in mammals (including humans). This phenomenon is referred to as lactational anestrus and probably accounts for the low frequency of adult male bears trailing a female during the mating season when she is still accompanied by cubs. Cessation of lactation and the hormonal changes the female experiences upon going into estrus go hand in hand, and result in not only receptiveness to the advances of a male but also eviction of her cubs.

After nursing, black bear cubs commonly retreat to safety in the crowns of forest giants to sleep.

As for all mammals, milk is a crucial element in the nourishment of cubs early in their lives. The very existence of mammary glands is one of the defining characteristics of mammals. While the cubs are still in the maternity den, milk is the only food available. But even after den emergence, nursing continues to be their most important source of nourishment for the next several months, although they will immediately sample whatever the mother consumes.

Lactation puts a tremendous strain on a female. She may lose as much as 40 percent of her body weight during hibernation. To raise her progeny and in addition to put on a layer of fat for the winter ahead, a female grizzly with cubs has to consume 20,000 calories per day. Not surprisingly, female black bears and grizzlies continue to lose weight – as much as 4.5 pounds (2 kg) per day – until late summer. In most areas, foods rich in fat or free sugars are not available in any quantity until the berries, fruits and nuts ripen.

· · ·

As the milk stops flowing, the cubs start to fuss, pull hard and bite on the nipples. They draw blood. No mother will take well to this kind of abuse. The female abruptly turns on her side and gets up. After a quick glance about, she guides her offspring over a little rise, then drops down into the next gully. They traverse a stand of lowland aspen and elms. Near an old hemlock the

Half lying, half sitting propped against a log, a grizzly nurses her young while keeping a watchful eye on her surroundings.

female sniffs some fallen logs and rips open a rotten stump. She has found an ant nest, and licks up the insects and larvae. One of the cubs discovers nearby the remains of a fox kill. A few days ago a grouse fell here, victim to the crafty hunter. Feathers and part of a wing are all that is left. With relish the young bear crushes the bones and chews on his find.

The female remains for only a short while in the shade below the conifer before she continues on. For almost an hour the family travels in a straight line through the forest, climbs a hill and then follows its crest. For the cubs this is a brand-new world; they have never been to this corner of their mother's territory. But soon excitement at the unknown is smothered by a growing weariness. They start to lag behind, sit down in protest and let out heart-rending whines. Again and again their mother waits, then walks back to offer encouragement. When the gentle approach loses it effectiveness, she nips the cubs on the back legs – an ursine version of the carrot-and-stick approach. Finally she stops underneath a tall fir. As if long-lost energy has been miraculously rediscovered, the cubs storm up the trunk into the very crown of the tree. As soon as they reach their lofty retreat they settle down, curl up next to each other in a fork between two branches, and fall asleep.

On the ground below, the female sits down, but soon she gets up again as

FACING PAGE: **Cubs are nursed from when they are born until they are forced into independent living, which can be as long as more than three years later.**

BELOW: **In the early summer of a cub's first year of life, nursing bouts may last as long as 15 minutes. Later, as they become larger, stronger and more efficient, they often suckle for less than four minutes.**

ABOVE: **A female grizzly charges a bear that has walked between her and her offspring. Communication between individuals is purposeful but tries to avoid injury. Even in this encounter the bears never touched.**

FACING PAGE: **Threat displays dominate arguments. The bigger the potential reward, the greater the chance of a fight.**

a scent catches her interest. Just 160 feet (50 m) from the fir she discovers the fresh droppings of another bear. She sniffs the pile intently, then moves over to a bed of grass. The telltale signs of a trespasser on her territory can be found everywhere. Not more than an hour ago another bear slept here. And she knows the scent – has known it for years. She glances back up at her progeny, hidden and safe from predators in their arboreal refuge. She appears to have made up her mind, and serenity gives way to an air of purpose. Her nose to the ground, she follows the scent trail down the hill into a ravine. Her stride lengthens and her step quickens as the odor gets stronger. She closes in on the other bear.

Next to a bubbling brook she finally spots a dark body deeply involved in play with a single cub. The sound of the water camouflages her approach. She is only 10 steps from the family when they finally notice her. The cub reacts with a scream of terror, standing up on its hind feet for a split second before galloping to the nearest tree as if pursued by the devil incarnate. The little claws grip the bark, the back feet push hard and in giant leaps the cub races to safety. The other female whirls around, ready to charge. But then she relaxes. Slowly the two bears approach each other and touch noses. They lick each other's face. For 15 minutes they romp around together in a display of affection and goodwill. Fights over territorial rights can be vicious, but not between these two. They are mother and daughter.

. . .

Territories are fixed areas that an animal or groups of animals defend against intrusion from other members of the species in order to have

Defending her cubs, a female brown bear charges a juvenile male. As the pursuer is larger than the pursued, this encounter could have ended fatally if the juvenile had not been able to outrun the protective mother.

exclusive use of its resources. A home range, on the other hand, defines the area an animal uses over the course of its life, but it does not defend its perimeters against intrusion by others of the species. Territorial behavior is found when the nutritional benefit of exclusive use of a resource is higher than the costs of defending the area. The food sources of a bear are generally highly seasonal and often widely spread. Particularly in a marginal habitat at the limit of their distribution, the animals may have to travel far to satisfy their nutritional needs at different times of the year. In addition, males typically occupy an area four to six times the size of a female's in order to include the home ranges of several females. During the breeding season a male covers a lot of ground to maximize his chances of finding a mate. As a result, the home range of a male grizzly may encompass 520 square miles (1,350 sq. km) in Canada's Barren Lands and on the North Slope of Alaska. Physically such a large area is not defendable, but a limited food source such as a small but productive berry patch or a carcass may very well be defended.

On the other extreme is the home range of coastal brown bears. Some females don't cover more than 9 square miles (24 sq. km) over the course of the year. The rich sedge flats and salmon runs enable the animals to make a living within a couple of drainage systems or even a single mountain valley. While the area might be defendable because of its size, the seasonal abundance of food renders defense of the resources pointless.

There is much to lose but no nutritional gain in staking out a territory. The amount of food consumable within a given time is determined by the surface area of the digestive system and the speed at which nutrients can

be transported and stored within the body. There is an upper limit. At some point the animal has to interrupt feeding and rest to digest, even if more food is available. Defending excess food costs energy and interrupts feeding. And most of all, every confrontation harbors the risk of injury.

For polar bears the concept of territorial behavior is nonsensical. Because of the unpredictability of ice conditions, an area of high productivity could turn into a polar desert the next year. Consequently polar bears are truly travelers of the Far North. The Inuit call them *pihoqahiaq* or *nanook*, both meaning "the ever wandering one." A male may cover 100,000 square miles (260,000 sq. km) over the course of a year in search of food and mates.

Black bears on average occupy the smallest home ranges. A female may only cover between 1 and 15 square miles (3–40 sq. km) annually, whereas males range from 8 to 40 square miles (20–100 sq. km). Over much of their range in North America, the productivity of their habitat is high enough to allow the animals to make a living within a defendable area. At the same time resources are for most of the year not abundant enough to exclude territorial behavior, so territoriality is observed in black bears. But it is important to differentiate.

While the definitions of "territory" and "home range" are clear, nature has proved unwilling to operate within the limits of these definitions. Scientists prefer to paint in black and white, and experiments are designed to provide concise answers. A gray zone makes analysis of the data difficult and clear statements and predictions impossible. But nature revels in shades of gray. In regard to territoriality in black bears, this is expressed in a flexible approach by both males and females – for instance in years of crop failures they often travel long distances across the territories of other bears to reach alternative feeding areas – and in the animals' gender-specific behavior.

Many female black bears are intolerant of strange females but not toward their own female offspring or strange males. After weaning, female black bears remain in the area they grew up in. Upon reaching sexual maturity they often establish a territory adjacent to their mother's. This probably increases the chances for survival of both, through reduced aggression. Male juveniles, however, are chased off, sometimes violently, if they don't disperse by themselves. In one instance the mother of a male cub reluctant to leave his familiar surroundings chased her offspring up the trunk of a white pine, got hold of its foot with her teeth and for a second was hanging free, dangling from her own cub's paw 65 feet (20 m) above the forest floor. If the cub had let go of his grip the episode would probably have ended with serious injury.

This intolerance toward male offspring increases the genetic diversity of a population by reducing the risk of inbreeding. For male juveniles the consequences are far-reaching. They are forced to vacate familiar surroundings with known resources at an age when they are still very vulnerable. Survival of males after weaning is hence much lower than for females. They are the ones that get into trouble with people and are responsible for most property damage. The solution offered by hunting lobbyists misses the mark entirely, as the large older male animals targeted by trophy-oriented "sportsmen" are not the ones causing the problem. In areas where bears and humans share the land, a young bear won't grow big by getting into conflict with people. If anything, hunting may worsen the situation by removing dominant males and increasing the population of inquisitive, undisciplined and potentially destructive juveniles.

Young male grizzlies and polar bears also tend to leave their childhood home for the uncertainties of the unknown. Juvenile brown bears travel sometimes hundreds of miles before being able to establish their own home range. A polar bear sighted near Thompson, Manitoba, almost 250 miles (400 km) from the shores of Hudson Bay, may be seen in this context.

The dispersal of males and the sedentary habits of females have an impact on the gene pool of a population. The result is simultaneously higher genetic diversity and also, as contradictory as it sounds, genetic uniformity. The nucleus of the fertilized ovum contains DNA from both parents. Every offspring represents a unique combination of the genetic material it inherits. Herein lies the benefit of sexual reproduction – every offspring is slightly different. These differences are the basis of natural selection of the fittest. Sexual reproduction is evolution in action – greater diversity of nuclear DNA helps a species to adapt to changes in the environment and counteracts tendencies toward concentration of genetic defects. But genetic uniformity in species with sedentary females comes in at a different level, and is not connected with nuclear DNA.

In all living organisms, apart from some bacteria, energy production is based on converting hydrated carbon molecules into carbon dioxide and water. This process takes place in almost all organisms, in the cell's mitochondrion. Mitochondria were originally independent organisms that entered into a symbiotic (mutually beneficial) relationship with another cell to form eukaryotes, on which all plants and animals are based. Because of their independent ancestry, mitochondria carry their own DNA – and this is where genetic uniformity comes into play.

Sperm fertilizes the eggs by providing chromosomes, but nothing else. The ovum provides maternal nuclear DNA and all the other elements of a vital cell, including the mitochondrion. As a consequence, mitochondrial DNA (mDNA) is inherited from the mother rather than being a combination of parental material. There is no reshuffling of the deck. Any changes come about slowly and occur solely through genetic drift. In bears, because their reproductive rate is slow compared to smaller vertebrates and because of the sedentary tendencies of females, mDNA is often extremely uniform. Its evolutionary longevity now allows mDNA to be used to determine the origin of populations and also to determine whether subspecies status is warranted by specific localized breeding groups.

Among polar bears, a very young species, there are no significant differences in mDNA among individuals in the entire world population of approximately 50,000 animals. Black bears, on the other hand, can be subdivided into 16 subspecies. They have been a species in their own right for much longer and don't roam as far, which has resulted in isolated distinct populations. There is some argument about how many subspecies of brown bears there are globally. Some scientists feel that all brown bears are members of the same subspecies, while others recognize four: two in the Old World and two in the New. According to the latter view, the Kodiak brown bear that inhabits the Kodiak archipelago in the western Gulf of Alaska is classified as *Ursus arctos middendorffi*, whereas all other brown bears in North America are called *Ursus arctos horribilis*. Ultimately this discussion is more of scientific interest than practical use. Even a specialist can't tell with certainty from a picture which is which.

Of greater importance to understanding bears and to bear conservation is a discovery in southeast Alaska. Analyzing the mDNA of bears on Chichagof, Admiralty and Baranof islands revealed that all the bruins inhabiting that area are descendents of one female. No females have successfully immigrated to the islands from the outside in thousands of years. In part this is probably because of the territorial behavior of the resident

A large male black bear seeks shelter from the heat of the day in a culvert. Black bears have even been known to den in drainage pipes underneath highways, apparently undisturbed by the constant rumbling of traffic above.

animals. But it also reflects the extremely slow overall expansion rate of a population into new areas, which is caused by limited migration of females. It exemplifies why the protection of females is crucial to long-term survival of bears. And it casts light on problems associated with fragmented habitats. While male juveniles are quickly able to reoccupy territory devoid of bears because of local extinctions, natural or human-caused, females don't follow.

In the European Alps a single male re-immigrated into Austria from Croatia in the mid 1970s. For 15 years the bear lived a solitary, secluded life without the general public's even being aware of his existence. Several

other male juveniles crossed the border during that period, but they were shot when they got into trouble with farmers and beekeepers. No females immigrated at all. Finally, after public debate and amid huge controversy, a recovery program resulted in reestablishment of a viable population through the capture of several females and their relocation into Austria. Grizzlies in the lower 48 states may experience similar problems. Wildlife corridors connecting core population areas may be insufficient to guarantee survival of small populations. If the initial number of females is small, accidental death, disease and human-caused mortality can quickly push a population below the threshold of recovery.

August

Chapter Seven

Streams of Life

Rain forest envelops the mountainsides. Western hemlock, Sitka spruce and Douglas fir form a dark green impenetrable canopy. Moss swathes branches in a thick, spongy layer; old man's beard, a lichen, drapes twigs like aged tinsel from a Christmas season long since past. Dozens of bald eagles perch in the crowns of the forest giants. In the dim light beneath the trees a large creek rushes to greet the ocean a mile farther downstream. Boulders channel the torrent into small falls and rapids. Below these rocky barriers, the river's surface is broken by fins. Pink salmon swim stacked up in the flowing water, scale to scale, a swirling mass of thousands of fish packed so tightly their bodies seem to merge into one.

A bear appears among the trunks of the spruce lining the small river. He stops at the bank and his eyes scan the water, focusing on the fish just a few feet out. The animal's pale coat gleams in the twilight. He seems to radiate brightness, alleviating the gloom of the rain-forest floor. The natives on this coast refer to him as the spirit bear.

. . .

To the general public he is known as the Kermode bear. To the taxonomist he is but a subspecies of the black bear, although a black bear trying his best to hide his true identity. His fur is creamy white, but Kermode bears are no albinos. They are a white color phase that is found along the British Columbia coast and in the southern part of the Alaska panhandle. Their best-known abode is Princess Royal Island, where about 20 percent of the black bears wander through the forests in fur coats of various shades of cream.

The spirit bear owes its existence to a rare recessive allele. Because of small founder populations and limited exchange of genetic material with the outside world, this gene has become widespread on islands. Two-thirds of the bears on Princess Royal Island are carriers of the gene. However, a cream-colored cub is born only if both copies of the gene on its chromosomes consist of the recessive allele. Thus – following Mendel's Law of heredity – if both parents are carriers, the mating of a black female and a black male may result in a mixed litter of both white and dark cubs. And a Kermode female will have exclusively black cubs if her partner is not a carrier.

The cream-colored bears seem perfectly able to hold their own against their black counterparts. Otherwise, natural selection would have slowly eradicated the gene from the population. However, there appears to be no advantage in being a lighter color; if that were the case, cream would be the dominant shade. Often, however, different fur color affects the survival chances of a bear and thus plays a role in the course of natural selection.

In spite of their common names, neither black bears nor brown bears can be identified solely by the color of their coat. The fur of black bears varies from shades of brown to blue-gray (the so-called glacier bear) to almost white. On the East Coast and along the rain-forest shores of the Pacific, black bears mostly live up to their name. With the exception of some island pockets, they are almost invariably black. Yet as you travel inland and south, brown becomes more frequent, then common, and finally prevalent.

This shift in the predominant fur color of black bears matches a shift in climate and vegetation patterns. The climate becomes drier and warmer; the forest canopy opens up. Black animals suffer more from heat stress than brown-colored black bears. This difference was demonstrated on a mountain ridge in New Mexico. Black-colored bears were found exclusively on the northern, cooler slopes. Not a single black animal frequented the dry, south-facing, sun-exposed side of the range – this was the domain of brown American black bears.

In terms of range of color, brown bears are like their cousins. However, in contrast to black bears, heat stress does not appear to effect coat coloration in these bruins, at least not within today's range of the animals. The typical inland grizzly in the Rockies is dark blond or gray, with darker legs and long gray guard hair. In the Far North, bleached by the midnight sun, brown bears are mostly a very light yellowish blond. On the coast, many animals are brown to almost black. It has been suggested that the dark coloration on the coast is food-related, in particular to fish oils. However, different populations with the same food source and separated by a mere 60 miles (100 km) of rugged coastline sometimes show opposing trends in fur color. Whereas in one population most bears are blond, they are dark brown, if not black, in the other, suggesting that genetics, not diet, determines hair color.

The absence of a clear correlation between coat color and environmental conditions in brown bears (as compared to black bears) may be a modern phenomenon. The distribution area of grizzlies in the lower 48 states is restricted to remote mountain ranges and high plateaus. Man has usurped all the prime habitat in the lowlands. When Lewis and Clark traveled across the prairies, they encountered grizzlies almost daily along the Missouri River in today's North Dakota and Montana. In their journals they often referred to them as "white bear." Many early biographers and analysts interpreted "white" as a loose description of blond or grizzled gray animals, similar to those found in Yellowstone and Glacier national parks today.

One of the great accomplishments of Lewis and Clark that set them apart from contemporary explorers was the precision with which they described the physical features of the landscape, plants and wildlife they encountered along their trek. This attention to detail makes their journals a valuable resource to this day. As the explorers fought their way up the Missouri,

FACING PAGE: **Pink salmon pool in a tidal slough before entering the freshwater stream to spawn.**

increasingly darker-colored and blond grizzlies were mentioned, and the white bear faded from view. The various members of the expedition each submitted their own reports. Never was a white bear in Lewis's diary described as a grizzly in Clark's report, and vice versa. The same holds true for all the journals. Thus it appears likely that there actually was a whitish grizzly out on the prairies – a region with hot summer weather and little shade, where overheating would pose a problem for bears and a light-colored coat would bring relief.

Bears are large, compact animals, and cold weather affects them little. Heat stress, on the other hand, is a problem they are all familiar with. A healthy male carries at least 1.5 inches (4 cm) of fat on his body, even after emerging from hibernation. As the fat is stored subcutaneously (under the skin), it serves as an excellent insulator. But insulators work both ways. While it blocks the cold from penetrating, fat also hinders heat from dissi-

A black bear carries a pink salmon away from the river to feed in private. Where salmon is available, black bears will join in on the food bonanza. In most parts of their range they obtain their prime fall weight, required for the denning period ahead, by gorging themselves on nuts and berries.

pating. Inuit elders in the Arctic tell of the old days when they pursued male polar bears on foot by running them down. The animals are so well insulated that they cannot move faster than 3 miles (5 km) per hour over any distance without their body temperature rising. An adult male will run a fever within a few minutes of trotting at just over 4 miles (7 km) an hour. Eventually the animal will collapse if it keeps up that pace.

A bear in prime condition is so well insulated that infrared pictures reveal no detectable heat. Temperature regulation is thus mostly an attempt to get rid of excess heat. Bears like to swim and lie in the water to cool off. They avoid the sun, resting during the warmest part of the day. Their hot spots are the muzzle, nose, ears, footpads and particularly inside the thighs and "armpits." Bears lie spread-eagled in their effort to dissipate heat; their groins and armpits are the only spots on the body that have little or no fur and no fat, as that would hinder movement. A network of blood vessels

Even among brown bears occupying the same area, color variations between individuals range from almost black to creamy white. Since the food sources are identical, it is clear that genetics, not diet, determines the coat color.

underneath the skin provides the body with heat vents. Under the skin in the shoulder region the animals also have a thin layer of muscles, richly supplied with blood vessels, that serves the same purpose.

. . .

For a couple of minutes the Kermode bear seems to stare longingly at the salmon in front of him. The water is too deep for a successful chase. The bear turns away from the river's edge and heads downstream, where the force of the water has piled uprooted trees along the bank. The trunks break the current so that a large, shallow eddy has formed in their shelter. In the slow swirl exhausted fish are resting, waiting to continue their journey to the upper reaches of the stream to spawn. Fishing is more likely to produce results here. Sure-footed, the bear walks across the slippery logs, then follows a large trunk until he stands above the water, watching the fish below him. Quietly he steps on a rock at the edge of the pool. Then he bends down quickly, grabs a fish with his teeth, and runs up into the trees with his catch. Unlike many brown bears, black bears never eat on the river, but carry the salmon as far as a mile into the forest to dine in private. This habit helps spread the wealth of the ocean among the timber – the bears' leftovers fertilize the woods.

. . .

For bears, dreams of gluttony come true during the salmon migration. Depending on the fish species, every catch represents a snack of 2,500 to 6,000 calories. Early on, when the vanguard of the salmon reaches the rivers – before the big schools of fish arrive – bears consume almost their entire catch. Apart from liver, jaws and gill plates, little remains for the gulls to fight over. Later, when fishing success comes fast and furious, they can afford to be choosy.

Some large males land as many as 50 salmon per day. The record for a brown bear is 89 fish in 10 hours. The species in question was chum salmon, which on average weigh more than 8 pounds (3.6 kg) each. It is physiologically impossible for a bear to consume 600 pounds (270 kg) of food in half a day, as its stomach capacity is normally 10 to 20 percent of its body weight. A large male polar bear may eat as much as 150 pounds (70 kg) in one sitting, but then the animal needs to rest and digest for several hours. Consequently the animals focus on the parts of the fish that are most nutritious.

A gram of fat yields over twice the calories of a gram of protein, so bears feed on the choice high-fat bits – skin, brain and caviar –

FACING PAGE: **Chasing after fish, a brown bear leaps into a creek. During the peak of the salmon run an adult bear may catch over 50 fish a day.**

ABOVE: **Comfortable even in temperatures well below freezing, a young polar bear enjoys the afternoon stretched out on his back among some willows.**

leaving the red meat behind. Polar bears do the same by feeding mostly on seal blubber. But leftovers don't go to waste. In the Arctic, polar bears will follow the tracks of a fellow bear, hoping the trail will lead to the remains of a kill. Dominant adult animals are often highly efficient and skilled in the hunt. They can afford to focus on the best parts and abandon the rest. Many, if not all, juveniles depend on the scraps that fall from the table of these individuals. And because they are young and still growing, they have a greater need for protein than older animals. The same holds true for brown and black bears along the salmon streams.

In other parts of their range, the rich resources that bears exploit may include plentiful crops of nuts and berries. The richer the fat content and the less effort required to collect the food, the better. Black bears focus on acorns and pine, hickory and hazelnuts where available. Grizzlies feed extensively on soapberries, which grow densely and are rich in fat. Under ideal conditions, daily rations amount to over 20,000 calories. With intake at such a gargantuan level, a bear is able to add 4.5 pounds (2 kg) to his body in a 24-hour period.

Excessive feeding and weight gain is called hyperphagia. While in humans this phenomenon is considered an eating disorder, in bears it is a necessity. The animals have to accumulate bodily reserves for hibernation

Obstacles in the migratory path of the salmon, such as shallow ripples or waterfalls, are favorite fishing spots. In these locations minimal effort meets maximum results.

and long periods of little or no food. On the coast a male brown bear may gain over 200 pounds (90 kg) during the salmon run. However, the pride of place for the highest weight gain is held by a 17-year-old female polar bear from the Canadian Arctic. When she was tranquilized and measured in November, the scales tipped at 218 pounds (99 kg). The following June she was caught again, and this time determining her body weight proved far more difficult, as she had filled in tremendously – the scales showed 904 pounds (410 kg).

If people abandoned themselves to cycles of fasting and feasting, the consequences would be serious, if not fatal. Yet what would amount to a dietary road to suicide for a human poses much less of a health problem for bears. Seasonal obesity is part of a healthy life for these animals. And how adipose (fatty) tissue is distributed is an important factor in obesity-related health issues. In male humans, fat is deposited in the abdominal cavity, which has the advantage of being near the center of gravity. As man developed in tropical Africa, fat deposits around the waistline allowed people to be physically active hunters without facing the problem of overheating. On the downside, however, obese men face a range of medical complications, including increased risk of heart attack. Women, on the other hand, mostly store fat subcutaneously on the hips and thighs, a pattern that is far more beneficial

Violent encounters are rare when nourishment is overabundant. This incident involving two males may be part of an ongoing struggle for dominance rather than a battle over food.

101

to general health. In bears the distribution of fat in both sexes is similar to the pattern for human females.

. . .

Over the next two hours the cream-colored male returns repeatedly to the river, catches a meal and retreats again without having his supremacy challenged by another bear. Two black juveniles drift through, but leave again when they spot the male. The stream is long and has many fishing spots, so there is little point in competing.

. . .

The largest animals occupy the best spots, and subordinate bears, either spatially or temporally, avoid animals higher in the hierarchy. In some areas the ranges of different species overlap. If brown and black bears share the same salmon stream, it is the brown bear that has choice of place. Because of their larger size and more aggressive nature, grizzlies displace their smaller cousins. On the shores of the Arctic Ocean and the adjacent tundra, polar bears and grizzlies sometimes meet. But here it is the grizzly that has to give up pride of place because of inferior size. Occasionally bears will even prey on their close relatives. Grizzlies have been observed killing black bears and feeding on the victims. The same has been noted for polar bears with grizzlies. However, as the areas of intersection are small, such cases are rare. Yet these instances of interspecies predation provide clues for analyzing present distribution patterns.

Black bears are probably more numerous in the Southwest now than they were two hundred years ago, when grizzlies still roamed those areas. The same is true for the prairies. In northern Labrador in the past few decades, black bears have extended their range into the treeless tundra, something they were able to do only after the grizzly was hunted into extinction in that region. For the most part, the species exclude each other. For example, grizzlies are not adapted to life in the forest. These animals are heavy and their claws are better suited to digging than to climbing. Important forest crops are thus not as accessible to a grizzly as to a black bear. In the subarctic, polar bears are unable to compete with grizzlies on land because of their size. The tundra simply can't sustain such a huge predator. Size is a knife that cuts both ways.

Challenged Monarch

Until recently, grizzlies and polar bears were seen as the undisputed sovereigns of the northern wilderness. The relationship between wolves and bears was regarded as clear-cut and written in stone: if a bear appeared on the scene, the wolf would recognize the bruin's or its white cousin's supremacy and surrender its prey. As more information became available, this picture started to look less likely. Bears and wolves were observed fishing next to each other without either one appearing to be dominant. One afternoon in Denali National Park in Alaska, amazed visitors watched from Polychrome Pass as a drama unfolded in the valley far below: a pack of wolves separated a grizzly from her offspring and killed a yearling cub. Wolves have been observed circling a polar bear female with a small cub in an attempt to lure the mother away from her young. Bones and hair from polar bear cubs have been found in wolf scat. In Katmai two wolves were watched as they snatched a cub of the year that trailed too far behind its mother.

Wolf predation on bear cubs may be more common than previously recognized. Against a wolf pack, a female bear may have little hope of successfully defending her progeny. Yet bears are still a dangerous quarry for wolves. They risk getting injured or even killed in their attempts to prey on cubs. Hence, wolves probably pursue bears only in times of acute food shortage or on a purely opportunistic basis. But the threat posed to cubs by a pack may explain why some bears, especially juveniles, appear nervous in the presence of wolves and flee when approached head-on.

At carcass sites, confrontations between adult bears and wolves seem to be won by the hungrier animal. However, individuals have been observed, only feet apart, feeding jointly on a moose kill.

September

Chapter Eight

The Hunter

In the Far North under an endless sky, a grizzly travels across the rolling tundra. The land is imbued with the flaming colors of fall; an unbroken ocean of red stretches to the horizon. No trees disrupt the smooth lines of the crests of hills. No groves of timber provide refuge from the incessant wind. A nip is in the air – the autumn breeze carries messages of the cold season ahead. In the Arctic and subarctic, fall is but a short interlude between the endless days of summer and the long nights of winter. After the caribou have started south on their trek to their winter range, after the migratory birds have departed, the tundra is embraced by the sounds of silence. Stillness lies heavy on the undulating land. To the casual observer snatching only a fleeting glimpse, this country appears devoid of life. Yet to the grizzly it is home. The treeless northern plains are where the animals evolved.

The bear is a straw-blond female, 15 years old. In the spring she chased off her previous litter of two and just a few weeks later mated with a large brown male. In her body new life has begun, but it waits in suspended animation for the hormonal cue to resume development. Continuation of the pregnancy will depend on the female's ability to accumulate enough bodily reserves to nourish both her and her offspring through the winter. To compensate for the physiological stress ahead, pregnant bears often enter the den in a hyperobese state, with their total body weight constituted of as much as 60 percent fat. They have little time to add fat deposits to their frame. In spring, after leaving the den, the female was lean; nursing had taken its toll. Although she was able to catch a few newborn caribou calves, she continued to lose weight until July. The land rejuvenates then, but unlike herbivores, bears can find little nutritional value in much of the new growth.

. . .

Bears are unusual carnivores. With the exception of the polar bear, their diet consists mostly of plant matter. Meat-eating carnivores always live between famine and feast. When they catch prey, it's a time of plenty. In the periods between meals, hunger reigns. The difficulty is that the animal has only a small window of time in which to catch something again before it is too weak to successfully pursue prey. Hunters cannot carry much fat on their body because it impedes their agility, speed and endurance. The additional weight slows them down; the insulating properties of fat cause overheating. To avoid food stress, many carnivores add vegetable matter to their diet. Foxes, for instance, feed on berries and fruit. Bears went one step farther and turned what was originally the side dish into the main course. To do that efficiently, they had to make some adaptations.

The development of teeth with complex surfaces plays a critical part in the success of mammals as an animal group. Most mammals rely on specialized teeth to manipulate food efficiently and prepare it for further digestion. Accordingly, dental structure reflects the diet of animals. Meat-eaters and herbivores face distinctly different problems. The teeth of a hunter have to hold on to prey securely, kill the victim and then butcher it. Plant matter, on the other hand, only has to be localized and then consumed. However, it is far more difficult to extract energy from plants than from flesh. The teeth of herbivores have sharp crests separated by valleys that shred vegetation into tiny pieces to aid further digestion. Often the teeth grow continuously to counter the heavy wear imposed by chewing fibrous plant material. The jaw joint allows for lateral movement to further facilitate the grinding of food.

Bears, as omnivores, differ in tooth and skull structure from specialist meat-eaters such as cats. They have the most cusped molars of any carnivore. Their carnassials, the teeth used to slice meat, are reduced in size. Relative to cats, the skull is larger and the snout longer in proportion to body size in order to provide space for more molars. All bears, with the exception of the sloth bear, have 42 teeth, including 10 molars specialized for mincing plant food. Large jaw muscles attach to the skull, resulting in the broad, massive head typical of bears.

With a burst of speed, a bear pursues a fish in shallow water. Despite the bear's fleetness and agility, more often than not its quarry escapes.

The most herbivorous of all bears, the giant panda, also has the most pronounced jaw muscles, which are required to crush bamboo. Consequently they also have the most dish-shaped face of all bears. Of all the ursines, the narrowest head in relation to body size belongs to the polar bear, which is also the most carnivorous species. The jaw joints of all carnivores resist lateral movement, probably as an adaptation to holding on to struggling prey. Bears still carry this evolutionary baggage and are hence unable to grind their food. Instead their upper and lower molars work like a mortar and pestle to squash the plant material.

While their dental adaptations improve digestive efficiency, bears still face a serious problem converting vegetable matter into nourishment. No mammal produces the enzymes required to break down cellulose, the main structural component of the cell walls of plants. Many herbivores rely on symbiotic microorganisms that dwell in special fermenting chambers in their guts to do the job. No member of the carnivores, including bears, has ever developed such chambers or obtained help from microorganisms in the digestion of plant material. In addition, because of the relative indigestibility of vegetables the intestines of herbivores are much longer than those of carnivores. The intestines of a cow measure 25 times the length of its body, while those of a cat are but four to five times the body length. Most bears have a gut that measures between six and ten times their body

BELOW: **Polar bears, being almost exclusively carnivorous, have larger canines than their close cousin the brown bear, which help them obtain a sure grip on their prey.**

BOTTOM RIGHT: **For a mountain grizzly, a large carcass is a much desired and fiercely defended resource.**

BOTTOM LEFT: **A juvenile chews on a skull he has found. Young, inexperienced polar bears depend on scavenging for survival.**

length. Ironically, the mostly vegetarian giant panda has the shortest intestines of all bears. Shorter intestines mean that the efficiency of a bear's digestive tract in regard to plant food is low – in a panda only 21 percent, whereas deer digest 60 percent of what they eat.

Brown bears and black bears compensate for their digestive handicap by being selective in what they eat and by consuming a wide variety of foods. Black bears along the West Coast, for instance, utilize at least 34 plant species. In the spring, however, while caribou and deer are starting to fatten up on new shoots, there is often little of nutritional value available to a bear. The animals feed on a salad buffet that provides them with fewer calories than they spend in searching for and eating comestibles. Individuals emerging lean from hibernation have been known to starve to death with a full stomach. Cubs and juveniles in particular fall victim to this energy imbalance.

As inefficient as the ursine digestive tract is when it comes to digesting plant food, the animals clearly show their carnivore heritage in their absorption of protein and fat. A polar bear living on a diet of marine mammals assimilates 84 percent of the muscle tissue and 97 percent of the blubber (fat) of its prey. On average these animals convert 92 percent of their food into energy.

. . .

The female grizzly is using the last days of fall to the fullest – this is her time to fatten up. Plants are carrying fruit in abundance. For the last three days she has fed almost without interruption on soapberries in a river bottom nearby, eating more than 200,000 berries per day. During the summer her appetite was excellent. On average she consumed over 29 pounds (13 kg) of food daily. Now, in the feeding frenzy prior to denning, that figure may triple. The berries also benefit from the attention they are receiving. Their germination rate is higher after passing through a bear's digestive system, and the bruins assist in dispersal of the plant.

As the bear crests a small rise, the shrill whistle of a siksik, or Arctic ground squirrel, erupts from a mound of dirt a hundred feet (30 m) to the right. The squirrel stands frozen on his hind feet, staring at the female. Then it utters another warning cry and takes off in a mad dash. The grizzly reacts immediately. Her slow-paced gait becomes a flurry of motion; focused intent replaces her seemingly apathetic demeanor of just moments before. She races after the gray rodent, staying in hot pursuit despite the squirrel's effort to shake off his pursuer with a couple of surprise 90-degree turns. A large moving mass turns with a wider radius than a small body, and the ground squirrel, by grace of the laws of physics, escapes with one last desperate leap into its den, vanishing from sight.

Immediately the female starts excavating the entrance. Chunks of dirt and rocks fly backward in a long arc from between her legs. Her powerful front paws, equipped with strong claws, dig into the ground with as much

Adult caribou (top), Dall sheep (center) and moose (bottom) have little to fear from a grizzly, but their newborn young are heavily preyed upon.

ease as a rabbit tunneling into a hill of sand. Grizzlies are built for digging. Their claws reach a maximum length of 6 inches (15 cm). Strong shoulder muscles provide her with sufficient force to move boulders several hundred pounds in weight without much effort. It is these muscles that form the grizzly's conspicuous hump, which is often used to identify the animal and distinguish it from the more arboreal black bear.

· · ·

Black bears don't rely on digging to obtain food as much as grizzlies. Their shorter, curved claws enable them to climb trees easily and search for food at lofty heights. This different use of the muscles renders their hump less pronounced. The same is true for polar bears, whose muscles are toned by swimming. But the hump is not a particularly useful identifying characteristic. In lean animals, particularly juveniles, the shoulder bones may protrude to give the appearance of a hump despite a lack of heavy muscle development. Body posture may hide a pronounced hump or emphasize a small one. Nobody would mistake a polar bear for another species, but to differentiate between black bears and brown bears it is best to focus on the facial profile, which is dish-shaped in grizzlies, while black bears have a straight roman nose.

· · ·

Within minutes only the female's hindquarters show above the rim of the crater she has created. Every few seconds she looks up to ensure that the

A six-pound salmon represents a food value of approximately 4,000 calories. To gain enough weight for the hibernation ahead, bears have to catch several each day for a period of weeks.

ground squirrel does not escape through one of several emergency exits. Foxes have been observed waiting next to a furiously digging grizzly, watching the back door for fugitives. And at times it is they who rake in the profit of the bear's hard work. There is no fox trying to snatch a morsel from this grizzly, though, and when the rodent tries to sneak out through a side entrance, the female pounces on it. Death comes quickly to the squirrel, with a bite to the head. The grizzly's actions impressively demonstrate that the fabled leisureliness and complacency of bears is mostly a myth.

. . .

The speed and explosiveness with which bears can act is often underestimated, as their walk appears laborious and their stature compact and heavy. Bears don't fit our image of a runner. But they can sprint at 30 miles (50 km) per hour, and a young animal unburdened by a layer of fat can keep up that speed for a mile or more. Even a world-class athlete would be left in the dust. The common belief that grizzlies cannot run fast downhill harbors no truth – a person cannot outrun a bear, regardless of terrain. Escape by running away happens by grace of disinterest on the bear's part, not the superior speed of the human. However, in most cases flight will trigger a chase response. Bears are still predators, although mostly opportunistically. They still have the instincts of a hunter. A bear that is unsure how to act in an encounter feels in control when the person takes to flight.

Grizzly and black bears can be highly effective predators of newborn

In the domain of the grizzly, salmon is usually unavailable as a food source. The animals rely on berries and the occasional windfall of an injured animal, such as this bull caribou, to fatten up.

ABOVE: **Juvenile, inexperienced bears often expend excessive energy in the pursuit of prey. Older, dominant animals are highly efficient in the hunt and rarely have to exert themselves.**

RIGHT: **Northern grizzlies depend more heavily on their hunting prowess than their southern counterparts, as the growing season is shorter and nutritious vegetable matter is less abundant.**

deer and moose calves, and they are able to bring down an injured adult animal. However, they are no match for the speed of a healthy ungulate. The reasons for this lie in body structure. As the animals grew larger during the course of evolution, their foot structure changed. To support the increased weight, they became plantigrade, meaning that they walk on the soles of their feet. Cats and dogs have digitigrade feet, in which only the toes touch the ground. This enables them to run faster by lengthening their stride. In contrast, nobody would call a bear fleet-footed.

Bears' legs are short by comparison, but they have a much larger range of motion than the limbs of typical runners. Heavily packed with muscles, the stout arms of bears are capable of producing great force. The mobility and strength of their limbs are imperative in their search for food and also in defense. Their feet are built to manipulate objects. The animals may not be able to escape danger by fleeing, but as a rule they are quite capable of repelling aggression with superior strength. And while not the fastest carnivore around, by adapting their strategy to take advantage of their physical abilities, bears can still be an extremely successful predator.

Polar bears depend on their hunting prowess because they cannot chase down prey. Though they are good swimmers, seals are faster and more agile in the water. But polar bears succeed by ambushing seals at their breathing holes. These animals live by their wits. Animal trainers and zookeepers regard bears as more intelligent than any other carnivore; in many areas their intellect is considered comparable to that of primates. It is those mental capabilities that allowed a female grizzly on the Barren Lands to catch 396 ground squirrels in a season, 357 of which were caught in the fall. At an average of 3,800 calories per animal, the nutritional value of her catch amounted to 22,000 calories per day.

In general, grizzlies in the Far North are more carnivorous than their relatives in the Rockies, possibly because of the shorter growing season in the Arctic. Yet even in areas such as Yellowstone, the animals show amazing flexibility in their diet and will utilize unusual food sources to supplement their vegetable menu. For some Yellowstone grizzlies, adult cutworm moths provide 90 percent of the animal's summer sustenance. Containing 72 percent fat and 28 percent protein, the insects are highly nutritious – although an acquired taste. Success in the game of natural selection depends on an animal's ability to secure enough food for survival. Bears excel at this game by feeding on a vast variety of food sources and quickly adapting to new ones when they present themselves. This is what compelled John Muir to state, "To the grizzly almost anything is food except granite."

Arctic ground squirrels have a pigment in the cornea that protects the eye from the harmful effects of ultraviolet (UV) radiation. Polar bears possibly have a similar adaptation: unlike humans they do not suffer from snow blindness.

October

Chapter Nine

Playtime

Hudson Bay is the most southerly Arctic body of water. It connects to the Labrador Sea and Davis Strait via a narrow entrance in the Far North. As a consequence, the bay is not caressed by warm ocean currents. Even in the summer the water temperature barely rises to a few degrees above freezing. Still, the warming sun melts the pack ice until by July only a few remnants are left hugging the northernmost shores of this land-bound sea.

About 4,500 polar bears call Hudson Bay home. The abundant seal population results in some of the highest concentrations of these supreme Arctic predators over their entire range. With the ice gone, the animals are stranded ashore, and a time of waiting begins for *nanook*. They rest in shallow daybeds along the coast to catch the cooling breeze of the ocean. Some dig dens down to the permafrost to get relief from the heat and mosquitoes. When fall comes and the temperatures drop, they start to migrate north, following the coastline until they reach Cape Churchill.

For most of its length, the Hudson Bay shore runs north to south in an almost straight line. Only between the mouth of the Seal River and Cape

FACING PAGE: Usually bears of similar age and size play together. Play bouts may last only a few minutes or may continue for over half an hour, after which the animals often retire to a shady spot to cool off.

BELOW: In coastal Alaska in the fall, as the days get cooler and the nights longer and bears have been gorging themselves on salmon for weeks, the animals can afford to doze away part of the day.

Churchill does the coast deviate from its northerly course and run east to west. Several major rivers empty into the bay at this point. The freshwater they carry to the sea dilutes the seawater, lowering its salinity. And as freshwater is lighter than saltwater, it sits like a blanket on top.

Wind affects the uppermost section of the water column. It catches the surface, creating ripples and waves. In western Hudson Bay, the weather comes out of the northwest. Consequently the surface water is pushed against the shore, and so is any ice that forms in the fall. Freshwater turns to ice at 32°F (0°C), whereas seawater freezes at 25°F (–4°C) because of the salt it holds in solution. The power of the wind and the physical properties of freshwater ensure that it is along this stretch of coast, between the Seal River and Cape Churchill, that the first ice in Hudson Bay forms while hundreds of polar bears wait on the shore for release from their terrestrial summer home.

. . .

Cape Churchill is a long spit of land protruding several miles into Hudson Bay. At its very tip a graveled beach ridge rises over 10 feet (3 m) above the tide line. Dozens of daybeds line its crest. Now, in late October, almost every one of these depressions is occupied by a large male polar bear. The spit is the domain of giants – females with cubs stay farther inland to avoid the dominant males. Juveniles occasionally head out onto the spit, only to make a hasty retreat and continue their walk westward, following the coast. For most of the day the large males rest. They are conserving energy, as they have done for the last four months. Ever since they got on land they have mostly fasted and lived off their fat deposits.

. . .

A polar bear's diet consists of 95 percent marine mammals. On the tundra there is little or nothing to feed on. Some individuals eat berries after they ripen, but the crops are insufficient to maintain such a huge animal. Nest robbing is unproductive, as most waterfowl eggs have already hatched. The caribou calves have grown and can now easily outrun a bear. In July thousands of geese are earthbound while the birds molt. However, an adult bear would have to catch one within 12 seconds or less to gain more energy out of the kill than is spent in the chase. So mostly the animals don't bother.

Predation depends on propitious circumstances. One year a young male was observed killing a healthy caribou after the Arctic deer made a fatal mistake, fleeing into a pond in its attempt to avoid the bear. The male jumped after it and easily overtook it in the water. But such kills are rare. The only reliable food source over the summer months and into the fall is kelp. The nutritional value of algae is probably negligible, but these primitive plants may contain essential trace elements such as iodine. A female was once observed diving repeatedly over 10 feet (3 m) to the bottom to retrieve kelp. She and her cub then selected the best bits and ate them.

Although the bears sleep away 20 hours of the day, they still lose 2.1 to 2.8 percent of their body weight every week.

. . .

In fall, as the days get colder and the end of their forced stay on land is approaching, the animals become more active. A large male wakes from deep slumber. Just lifting his head seems an effort. With beady black eyes he glances about. Then, with a wide yawn, he stretches and slowly rises to his feet. As if contemplating every stride, he walks in a leisurely manner over to a vacant daybed 20 feet (6 m) away and thoroughly sniffs the sand.

Just a few steps farther another male notices the movement and gets up as well. His head held low and ears pointed forward, he ambles toward the other bear. Caution dictates behavior as the animals meet. The approached bear backs off slightly to signal a nonconfrontational disposition. He too lowers his head and then presents his flank in a display of size. A few feet apart both males size each other up, then lift their heads to sniff the air. They are each other's equal in weight and shoulder height. Old scars, the insignia of participants in the mating game, crisscross their noses. A dark patch of exposed skin graces the shoulder of one male. The large wound from a fight over a female has healed well, but he will carry the mark for the rest of his life. As battle-proven as both animals are, there is no aggression in their actions now, only a careful evaluation of mutual intent.

As one male sits down on his rump, the other takes his posture as an invitation to approach. The males sniff noses. Then both open their jaws and gently mouth each other. Slowly the standing male pushes against his

Bears of all ages play: the younger they are, the more frequently and intensely. But even as adults, full-grown males indulge in the joys of a friendly wrestling match. In the absence of competition for mating privileges or food, the mostly solitary bear becomes quite social.

new-found friend, rolling him over. Quickly the wrestling match gains speed. Entangled, they bite neck and ear and grab a foot. After a five-second interlude to catch their breath, they jump on top of one another. Then they rise on their hind legs and push and shove in an attempt to unbalance their opponent. For 20 minutes the bears play, oblivious to their surroundings. Eventually a third bear of similar size joins them. Finally, exhausted, the males lie spread-eagled in the snow, panting heavily. Despite little nicks and drops of blood staining muzzles and shoulders, they give clear indication of a good time had by all. For the next several weeks a bond connects the three males. They rest together between bouts of play and go their separate ways only as the ice forms.

· · ·

Bears are commonly thought of as asocial and solitary animals. Friendly wrestling matches and temporary friendships between individuals do not fit the image of an animal that lacks the need or capacity for social interactions. Yet such scenes of mutual goodwill are neither rare nor restricted to polar bears or Churchill. Juvenile and also adult brown bears play, at

BELOW: **Siblings are the most frequent playmates, even after the protective shelter of maternal wings has lifted.**

FACING PAGE: **During the salmon run bears show little interest in other potential food sources and mostly ignore human anglers. Their attention is focused single-mindedly on fish and little else.**

times intensely, for hours. The same is true for black bears. Generally speaking, all bears play – the younger they are, the more intensely. Usually wrestling matches involve individuals from the same cohort: adult males grapple with other dominant males, juveniles play with juveniles, and cubs tussle with their siblings. In bear families, in the absence of a sister or brother the rule of equal size in a wrestling match is broken – the mother serves as a willing surrogate playmate. Apart from bouts within a family group, the criteria that have to be met for play to occur are a location where bears congregate and a lack of competition for mating rights and food. The assertion that bears, particularly grizzlies, are asocial stems in part from observations of the animals in marginal habitats, where the concentration of animals is low and competition for resources is high.

Play behavior paints a far more sympathetic picture of the animals by demonstrating that interactions between individuals are not inevitably antagonistic. Neither is a human–bear encounter unavoidably a confrontation. All too often curiosity is interpreted as aggression. These seemingly contradictory traits – of solitary animals behaving socially and of playful curiosity intermixed with aggressive response to external triggers – demonstrate the plasticity of the bear's behavioral repertoire. And it is this rich behavioral gamut that enables the animal to survive in a wide variety of conditions.

Because of habitat constraints, bears infrequently encounter other bears over much of their range. Interactions between individuals are thus minimal and, with the exception of the mating season, mostly antagonistic. Yet in situations of high bear density, a rudimentary social structure develops to enable coexistence in close proximity. Associations between the animals, with the exception of

family units, remain loose and temporary; they don't form herds or packs. For permanent social groups to evolve, the benefits must compensate for the drawbacks. The major costs of living socially are that food has to be shared and also that mating rights, particularly for subordinate males, are restricted. The survival and procreation of the group supercede the interests of the individual. The benefits consist of support in raising offspring, defense of group members and – among predators – cooperative hunting.

A cost-benefit analysis makes it evident that group living does not pay off for a bear. The only natural threat to an adult ursine is another bear. As a full-grown animal can hold its own against another of its species, living in groups does not provide a sizable advantage. While the bears would benefit from group hunting in a situation such as beluga whales trapped in a closing lead or a bison wounded in a mating battle, these events are isolated and occur at unpredictable intervals, so social units never evolved. Size of prey and the seasonality and spotty distribution of resources counteract any tendencies toward cooperation. As a consequence, adult bears always act as individuals, never as a team.

The only permanent social structure in bear society is a female with cubs. Occasionally juveniles will group together before reaching sexual maturity. Association with others means safety in numbers, and jointly they are able to compete for a fishing site or even push another bear off an otherwise unavailable kill. But mostly the dominant animal in these temporary relationships claims the food for himself. The subordinate profits by obtaining leftovers. And in a serious confrontation, despite the bravado and displays leading up to the event, it is again everyone for himself.

The predominantly solitary existence of bears has an impact on the communication skills of the animals. As social contact between individuals is relatively small, there is little need for communication beyond the very basics. Thus the animals lack a complex body language, and the ability to vocalize is limited to a narrow range of sounds – in absence of

On the Hudson Bay shore, polar bears often form lose associations. Play is frequently initiated among members of these groups. As the animals know each other, there is no need to confirm the good intentions of the wrestling partner, and play appears carefree, with no holds barred.

demand, the morphological features necessary never evolved. The requisite muscles for facial expressions are poorly developed. The ears are small and unsuited to conveying visual signals. And the tail is but a short stump, no better at displaying a message.

These physical limitations mean that communication between bears is more straightforward than in many other animals; it lacks nuances and intervening steps are frequently skipped. Yet bears do give signals, although often they are misinterpreted or not recognized as such. Nervous bears frequently yawn, which is regarded by humans as a sign of boredom. A bear experiencing extreme stress may foam at the mouth, an indication that the animal is walking the thin line separating flight and fight. Such signals demonstrate that the so-called magic circle of a bear – a personal space of individual diameter – has been violated. Any transgression of a bear's private sphere results either in the animal's withdrawing or in force-ful removal of the intruder. The size of this private sphere depends on

Juveniles regard every novel object as a potential toy that requires thorough inspection. Tug-of-war is a favorite pastime.

ABOVE: Two black bear cubs take a pause in a game of king of the tree. Fear of heights is unknown to them: they wrestle and pull at one another as if they were on level ground.

FACING PAGE: A 10-month-old cub is fascinated by the activities of a downy woodpecker. Curiosity and play are integral to the success of bears as a species. It's the playful investigation of the unknown that renders them so infinitely adaptable.

many factors, such as physical conditions, the animal's previous experience and also genetic predisposition.

As they live in a dynamic environment and utilize a vast range of resources that are different for every animal, the experiences a bear accumulates throughout its life are unique to each individual. Part of their genetic inheritance is the capability of bears to learn and to solve problems. In other words, the animals are highly intelligent. But intelligence and moodiness seem to go hand in hand. Every bear is a product of its past, present and genetic makeup; every individual has a character of its own. As a result, different animals react differently to environmental stimuli. And depending on its emotional state at the time, the same bear may display diametrically opposite behavior in similar situations. This does not mean they are unpredictable, but simply that they are not machines.

The general tendency of bears to act as individuals stands in stark contrast to social play behavior. Indeed, one would expect that their solitary habits would preclude such activities. However, play is also an expression of an inquisitive mind. A playful attitude extends beyond interactions with another individual to include investigation and manipulation of objects. Bears of all ages thoroughly inspect unknown items in their environment, the more so the younger they are. In experiments in zoos, the animals investigated novel objects such as toys in their enclosures more intensely and for longer than primates. Some individuals developed complex games to keep themselves amused. This exploratory behavior is part of the animal's survival strategy, a characteristic that has a direct bearing on the success of the bear as a species, for a close inspection of surroundings may reveal a food source thus far unexploited.

The innate curiosity of bears extends beyond the inanimate to the animal's cohorts. Here the benefit is acquisition not of nourishment but of social skills. In play the animals learn to assess and interact with possible competitors. Social bonds are reinforced and social behavior is refined. In addition, engaging in games of tug-of-war is a way to practice survival skills. And for cubs, wrestling matches with siblings or the mother promote healthy bone growth. Play in bears, as in humans, is a serious activity with a purpose, even though its function may not be immediately apparent to the observer. But purpose does not automatically eliminate enjoyment. Watching the animals makes it difficult not to believe that they sometimes play for no other reason than sheer fun.

November

Chapter Ten

The Long Sleep

A heavy curtain of snow drapes a veil across the land. In the forest the trunks of pine, spruce and fir appear like ghosts in a surreal dream. Within hours a thick white carpet has hidden the brown earth beneath, insulating the soil from the cold. The first frost is already several weeks old. Ice skins the lakes. But up to now, except for an ephemeral white dusting, the undulating hill country had not yet received its warm winter coat.

Next to a fallen forest giant sleeps a young male black bear. Snowflakes dot the male's fur like icing sugar. He doesn't mind the freezing temperatures nor does he feel the sting of the cold. A thick layer of fat and his dense fur are ample protection. Behind him looms the dark maw of the entrance to his den. The male has enlarged a small cavern between the roots of the dead tree to fit his body. He carried in vegetation – leaves and dry grass, moss and some pine boughs – to line his bed a foot (30 cm) deep. After the completion of his home renovation project the animal slipped into lethargy, spending most of his days resting. His only food intake consists of some grass, although just a few weeks back he was feeding almost nonstop on pine nuts and acorns. When the nuts became sparse and a strong frost killed the last berries, he went in search of a winter domicile.

. . .

Most bears are faithful to their denning area but not to the den itself, as they often collapse over the summer. Frequently female coastal brown bears, but also pregnant polar bears, will occupy dens within close proximity of each other, sometimes only 30 yards (27 m) apart. As female cubs usually remain in the general neighborhood where they were born, the clustering of maternal dens can be seen as an expression of loyalty to the wintering area of their youth.

It is not the chilly temperatures that drive black bears and brown bears into hibernation; it's a lack of food. Polar bears, with the exception of pregnant females, don't retreat from active life in winter, as marine mammals are still available as prey. However, this is an oversimplification. The pattern of seasonal food shortage for polar bears is very different from that of black and brown bears. Generally polar bears experience periods of low availability of prey during the summer months.

Research has shown that polar bears are physiologically in a state of hibernation when they are shore-bound during the summer. They may not enter a den and they keep on moving about, but their metabolic rate is reduced. It appears, though, that while the metabolism is slowed down it is

ABOVE: **Polar bears, with the exception of pregnant females, do not hibernate, but roam across the sea ice in winter in search of food.**

FACING PAGE: **A young male carries on his back the mark of an encounter with another bear, probably a large male. The animals are amazingly resilient and can survive serious injuries if given sufficient time to heal.**

still higher than that of a hibernating black bear or grizzly. It resembles more closely the physiological state of the latter animals upon entering or leaving the winter home. This transition period has also been dubbed "walking hibernation." The interesting part is that polar bears are able to switch readily between an active state and walking hibernation. A bear that has access to food in the summer changes his physiological condition from hibernating to non-hibernating. Some scientists believe that polar bears perform that biochemical feat throughout the year. In a blizzard in the depth of winter the animals will hunker down and lower their metabolic rate to conserve energy. Black bears and grizzlies are apparently unable to do this. If they don't feed in the summer, they starve.

This leaves the question of what causes a black bear or a grizzly to go into hibernation. The internal chemical substance that causes bears – and apparently other hibernators such as the ground squirrel – to lower their metabolic rate and slip into hibernation is called hibernation induction trigger (HIT). Except for the polar bear, release of this hormone seems to be associated with temperature and photoperiod (hours of daylight). In zoos, black bears and grizzlies lose their appetite in late fall and become somewhat lethargic. However, they will remain active if they continue to be fed and if no den is provided. Hibernation in these two species is probably triggered by a combination of food scarcity and environmental conditions. Polar bears, however, have evolved one step further. For them the switch occurs solely as a result of unavailability of food.

The data available suggests that in grizzlies and black bears environmental conditions result in walking hibernation only. It is shortage of food that causes them to den up. In both species, depending on the availability of resources, some individuals are intermittently active in the winter. On Kodiak Island in southwestern Alaska, in mild winters the dominant males never retreat to protected quarters to renounce the outside world for a few months. Instead they keep on searching for food along the tide line and bed down underneath a bush for a few weeks during the worst of the season. In other areas on the Alaska Peninsula, Coho salmon spawn in

In late fall the first animals to retreat to their dens are juveniles, pregnant females and mothers with their cubs. The last to go into hibernation are dominant males.

January and February. And with a fish run waiting to be exploited, some bears take advantage of the opportunity.

Similarly, some black bears in the southern part of their range remain active in winter. Yet they show little exuberance during that time. Instead they are relatively sedentary, making short trips to feed but at other times appearing extremely lethargic. Individuals prowling for food in the winter are almost exclusively adult males, even though they are the individuals in the population that are in the best condition and in the least need of nutrition. However, even where food is available in the winter, it is a premium commodity. Large males are the only ones able to contend successfully for the limited resources available. This is also the reason for the staggered exodus from active life in fall. Depending on gender, family status and age, bears enter their dens at different times that reflect their varying abilities to compete. Pregnant bears and females with cubs belong to the vanguard. They are followed by sub-adults, then adult females without progeny. The last to bed themselves down for the long sleep ahead are the dominant males.

The number of weeks or months slept away in a den varies significantly within a population, and also among different areas. In some populations at the northern extent of their range, grizzlies and black bears spend over half their lives in hibernation. The record is held by a female grizzly on the North Slope of Alaska that remained in her den for eight months every year.

• • •

As the sun sets, the black bear, now covered in snow, rises. He shakes thoroughly, then stands motionless on all fours for a couple of minutes as if to say good-bye to the outside world. Finally he turns around and crawls into his den, not to reappear until spring.

• • •

Bears often enter the den under cover of a storm, possibly to hide their tracks leading to it. Bears in a den are vulnerable, and predation on denning bears has occurred, particularly by large males. Yet the animals inside are not defenseless. A ground squirrel or marmot unearthed in the middle of winter is cold to the touch and immobile. The animal is helpless and unable to move. Bears in a den, on the other hand, will look back at an intruder. When a heart monitor was attached to a female with cubs, it was observed that even in the middle of winter her pulse quickened when people approached the den – the animal was aware of what was going on outside. The metabolic rate of a bear in hibernation slows by half, the heart rate drops from 50 beats a minute to 10, and the body temperature falls from 98.6°F (37°C) to between 86°F and 93°F (30°C–34°C). Yet every day a large male or a pregnant female still burns over 4,000 calories, or a pound (0.5 kg) of fat. During hibernation the animals lose between 15 percent and 40 percent of their body weight.

Because of their high base metabolic rate compared to species such as

ground squirrels, bear hibernation was often referred to in the past as winter rest rather than winter sleep. Bears were considered to be "inferior hibernators." This line of thought has long since been abandoned. Today biologists differentiate between small and large hibernators. The body temperature of a hibernating rodent chills to within a few degrees of freezing or may even dip below the freezing point, and its heart reaches only 1 to 2 percent of its summertime performance. However, every two weeks the animals start shivering violently to raise their core temperature. They wake up, urinate and defecate, drink a little bit and have a snack, and then they lie back down. This fortnightly event is extremely costly in terms of calories burned, but it is necessary for the animals in order to avoid poisoning themselves. The waste products of metabolism must be removed from the body.

For bears the rodent type of hibernation is not an option – the animals are simply too large. A bigger and more compact body cannot warm up and cool down quickly. The two-week cycle would be highly inefficient for a bear. More important, however, is that larger animals have longer gestation periods. Fetus development in a bear would abort if it weren't for its higher metabolic rate in hibernation. This doesn't mean that bears are inferior hibernators. On the contrary, they are highly adapted. In contrast to rodents, bears do not drink or eat during hibernation; neither do they defecate or urinate.

Lack of food, not the prevailing temperatures, drives bears into hibernation. In some areas with winter salmon runs the animals are active even during the coldest months.

Hibernation as it occurs in bears is physiologically impossible for rodents, or for humans for that matter, regardless of whether the person is lean and mean or built like a sumo wrestler. Energy supply and consumption are not the issues. Because bodily functions are slowed but not dramatically reduced, a number of problems arise that are more difficult to solve than matters related to fuelling the metabolism.

No living being is ever a finished product, but instead is continuously being remodeled according to current physical stresses. Muscle tissue is being either built up or reduced. Bones are either strengthening or thinning out and weakening. A bedridden person will suffer from muscular atrophy within a short time. Weightlessness causes the bones of astronauts to become fragile during lengthy flights in space. Bears stay curled up inside their small dens for months, yet their muscle mass remains constant or shows only a gradual decline, and their bones remain strong even in the absence of physical strain. Most other mammals show a continuous loss of body protein when fasting. How bears maintain bone density is unknown.

It is hormonally related, but how the biochemical processes work has yet to be discovered.

Maintenance of muscle mass is accomplished through an almost complete recycling of metabolic waste products into proteins. This also prevents metabolic waste from accumulating and reaching toxic concentrations. We need to drink and urinate to flush nitrogen compounds out of our system. Otherwise, altered pH levels in the cells would cause our metabolism to collapse. The kidneys are in charge of detoxifying the body, and people with kidney disease or kidney failure depend on frequent dialysis to stay alive. If we could understand how bears recycle their metabolic wastes, the lives of many would be improved.

Their physiological feats have made bears popular research subjects for human medicine. The results of this research may provide new medications and treatment for diseases such as osteoporosis and kidney failure. The discovery of the hibernation induction trigger (HIT) may prove to be a milestone in organ transplants. Tissue deterioration renders donor organs useless

At the southern limit of their range, after the sea ice melts, polar bears are held prisoners on land. Nursing females lose over two pounds (1 kg) per day during the summer months. They wait eagerly for the ocean to freeze again in the fall so they can return to their hunting grounds.

within 16 hours at the most. As many as 20 percent of donor organs have to be discarded before they ever reach the operating room. However, if the donor organs are perfused with HIT, tissue deterioration is slowed down threefold. There are other possible applications for HIT as well. A monkey injected with HIT fell asleep for six hours, its heart rate and body temperature dropped, and its appetite was depressed for almost a week. This suggests that probably all mammals, including humans, are responsive to HIT. If so, the hormone might prove useful in treating various conditions such as obesity and insomnia.

The popularity of bears in modern medicine is a product of the recent past. In traditional Oriental medicine, however, the bear has played an important role for over a thousand years. In China the bear's gallbladder was, and in many places still is, the treatment of choice for jaundice, abdominal pain and distention—all symptoms caused by liver and bile duct diseases, in particular, gallstones. It is tempting to banish claims of the healing powers of gallbladders into the realm of fable. But research has revealed that the old Chinese were right – gallbladder tea works. Bear bile contains a substance called ursodeoxycholic acid (UDCA), which will dissolve certain kinds of gallstones without causing any substantial side effects. Today UDCA is produced synthetically for use in hospitals and as a prescription drug.

The demand for bear gallbladders, however, has not been slackened by advances in pharmacy. In the Far East the authentic product is credited with higher potency. In China, Korea and Japan dried and ground-up bear gallbladders sell for over $50 a gram. As result, a lucrative traffic in bear parts has developed. Some estimates suggest that many as 100,000 black bears are poached every year in North America to supply the Asian market. In 1985 an Air India Boeing 747 flying from Canada exploded in midair, killing all 329 passengers. In the cargo com-partment were two suitcases filled with the gallbladders of approximately a thousand black bears. In the Far East the shipment would have had a street value of a million dollars.

It isn't only the gallbladders that poachers are after – bear paws are almost as valuable. In Japan a cup of bear-paw soup fetches several hundred dollars. The watery broth is reputed to confer general well-being and health. During the 1988 Seoul Olympic Games, the reputed medicinal value of bear meat compelled the Korean government to fly in 30 live Asiatic black bears from Thailand to feed its athletes, in the belief that their meat would enhance performance. The bear's reputation has benefited greatly from recent discoveries of modern medicine, but the Oriental market for bear parts based on traditional medicine has become an issue of major concern, particularly for black bear populations.

· · ·

As the young male sinks into a deep sleep, the entrance to the den slowly fills with snow and all evidence of his presence is erased. The fight for survival is on hold until next year.

December

Chapter Eleven

Restless Giants

In the far southern part of Kodiak Island, in a bay overlooking Shelikof Strait, a large male brown bear follows the edge of the steep beach. The wind howls in a fury. Out on the strait, the forces of storm, current and tide interact violently until breakers pile up over 30 feet (10 m) high, making Shelikof Strait one of the roughest and most treacherous bodies of water in the world. The wind catches the foam of whitecaps and blows the spray in wisps across the surface of the ocean. A transition zone belonging to neither the sea below nor the sky above blurs the division between the elements and robs the waves of definition and contour. On shore the male is buffeted by the gale and soaked by the salty mist. The water turns to ice in his fur, encasing him in frozen armor. Even for a bear, this is a miserable day for a seaside stroll.

For the past several days the animal had been resting behind a bluff. But then the smell of rotting flesh caught his attention and he decided to investigate. The bear is an old individual, long past his prime. He has seen more than 30 summers in his capricious life. In years past he was the seldom-contested sovereign of the Ayakulik River, fishing for salmon in the most productive spots. Today he avoids all confrontations, having slipped far in the hierarchy. Yet despite his loss of authority and the resulting inability to defend the best fishing locations against younger, more domi-nant boars, he has been able to maintain his weight until this season. Exceptional fish runs have provided food in surplus.

· · ·

A male brown bear in the wild is considered old when he reaches his early twenties. Not many walk a few tentative steps into the fourth decade of life. The record age for an adult male in the wild is 34. Females on average have a higher life expectancy than males. Generally they live into their late twenties and, if their physical condition allows it, they continue to give birth to litters even at that ripe age. Their greater life span is associated with size. Being smaller, they require less food to sustain their body, which puts them less into competition with their fellow bruins when resources are scarce.

In captivity, animals live longer because of an absence of competition, a balanced diet and the assistance of a veterinarian. The oldest brown bear in a zoo had to be euthanized at 47. It was a female, and she had her last litter at 42. Both black bears and polar bears also reach their forties in zoos. The oldest black bear died at 44 years of age, and the oldest polar bear at 41.

In the wild, the life expectancy of a black bear is roughly equivalent to that of a grizzly.

Polar bears in their natural environment, however, don't hang on quite as long as their cousins. Very few males see their twentieth birthday. On average they live into their late teens, while females make it to their early twenties. The reason for polar bears' lower life expectancy is the greater physical demands on the animals as compared to both grizzlies and black bears. Every season they travel as much as several thousand miles in search of food. As hunters they depend on stamina, speed and agility. As they grow beyond their prime, prey escapes more frequently and the animals eventually starve.

· · ·

The old male on the beach has seen better days. His body is failing him. He is plagued by arthritis – every move is painful. Old wounds have left their mark. His right front foot is crippled because broken bones in his wrist and palm, the result of many fights, never properly mended. A huge scar disfigures his saddle. In his prime he weighed in at nearly 1,500 pounds (700 kg). His belly almost dragged on the ground. His hips were massive. Over 4 inches (11 cm) of fat covered his upper thighs. Now his legs are skinny and appear barely able to support his weight, despite the fact that he has slimmed down to less than 900 pounds (400 kg). His teeth have started to give out too. His molars are but brown stumps, their roots exposed. His

Rodents chew on bones to obtain calcium. Since bears' calcium requirements are met by their regular diet, this animal's interest in a moose skull is based merely on curiosity about the object.

As bears don't live in packs or herds and cooperation between individuals is virtually nonexistent, their communication is rudimentary and skips steps, which has earned the animals a reputation for being unpredictable.

canines are worn down. Every bite hurts. In the summer he was hardly able to rip through the skin of a fresh salmon. In the fall he fed on rotting fish carcasses, but the nutritional value of spawned-out salmon is small.

Juvenile bears show little respect now. To tease him, they walk up to within a few yards, fully aware that he can't and won't chase them. Just a few years ago they would have given him a wide berth. Among bears there is no respect or sympathy for elders. In years past he left the lower river and the coast in November and went inland before the winter storms hit. This fall his fat reserves are depleted. He can't hibernate, and the tide line is the only place left where food can sometimes still be found.

The old male, guided by a faint scent trail, continues his march into the storm until he reaches a spit assailed by the pounding waves. At the very point of the sand bar, half submerged, a dark body is being carried up to shore by the breakers, then pulled out again as the water recedes between swells. It is a gift from the sea. A dead bull moose is being washed up on the beach. Moose don't occur on Kodiak Island, but they are plentiful on the mainland, 27 miles (43 km) across Shelikof Strait. Occasionally during the rut, when testosterone runs freely, some bulls underestimate the width of a bay and drown in the attempt to swim across, their huge antlers too heavy to hold above the water. The current carries them out into Shelikof Strait and sometimes deposits them on the opposite side.

It is not the first time that dead moose have been found on the southwest corner of Kodiak, but it's a lucky find for the male. It takes him but a few minutes to drag the carcass ashore. Despite his emaciated body, he is still incredibly strong. For two days the old bear feeds on the moose. Because of his rotting teeth it is a struggle, but he still manages to consume many pounds of fat and meat. After each meal he covers the carcass with sand and then beds down on top.

• • •

Both grizzlies and black bears bury carcasses to hide the meat from jealous eyes and noses. But polar bears rarely bother to cover up a seal kill. The size of the prey and the frequent availability of seals make such measures unwarranted. Mostly polar bears stuff themselves to the gills and then abandon the remains. Other bears, Arctic foxes, ravens and seagulls clean the plate quickly. In fact, every bear is the focus of an entire community of scavengers. Arctic foxes in the winter depend on polar bears for their survival. They even become quite possessive about their provider and chase competing foxes away.

• • •

On the morning of the third day another bear approaches the old male as he sleeps next to the dead moose. The putrid stench of the carcass has drifted far inland on the ocean breeze and lured the newcomer to the shore. The animal is a large, healthy male in his prime. With every step he exudes self-assurance and an air of supremacy. Confident in his strength and status, he doesn't even slow down to assess the situation when he becomes aware of the other bear, but walks straight up to the mound of sand and flesh.

The old male wakes up startled as he hears the steps nearby. He gets up on all fours and faces his opponent with his head held low and ears back. His hind legs are spread wide and his feet are dug into the sand like a runner at the ready in the starting blocks. His mouth is open; foam covers his lips. With a roar he launches toward the other bear, but stops short after two steps. His display doesn't much impress the dominant male. Both stand

To defend her offspring, a female with yearling cubs charges a male polar bear. With nowhere to hide on the open ice, the safest place for the young is right next to their mother. In contrast, black and brown bear cubs flee from a fight.

ABOVE: **In a bear's world, bigger is better. The top positions in the hierarchy are held by the huge adult males. Fights to establish rank are rare, as dominance displays are usually sufficient to discourage a subordinate animal.**

FACING PAGE: **A standing bear is not an animal about to charge, but rather one that is unsure and slightly nervous about its surroundings: it's trying to get a better look.**

motionless just 6 feet (2 m) apart in a face-off. Then the new arrival turns sideways and shows his bulk. After a few tense seconds the old male retreats a step and sits down. His challenger walks over to the carcass and starts feeding, his back turned to the old male. He is totally ignoring the other bear. The hierarchy has been established, and there will be no further argument.

• • •

Attacks from behind occur only when animals seek refuge in flight. A challenger will even move around a bear that is presenting his back to approach again from the front. Interactions are based on communication, which demands face-to-face contact. You can't communicate with your opponent's behind.

Confrontations are governed by the position in the hierarchy of the individuals involved, the physical condition of the animals and the value of the object of desire. The more scarce a resource, the higher the competition for it. The position of a bear in the hierarchy is determined by size and

Yawning is often a sign of mild stress rather than boredom. Very excited bears may foam at the mouth, a clear signal to give the animal a wide berth.

aggressiveness. The huge adult males claim the very top ranks. On the ladder of dominance they are followed by maternal females, which owe their elevated position to their tendency to behave aggressively whenever they perceive their cubs to be in danger. The very bottom ranks are held by three- and four-year-old independent sub-adults. But the hierarchy is not always apparent, even when bears congregate in large numbers in a small area. Dominant bears display intolerance toward subordinate animals when the food supply is restricted. At the peak of the salmon run, when the waters abound with fish, or on a whale carcass in the high Arctic, bears of different size are occasionally observed feeding peacefully next to each other.

Even if competition is high, confrontations rarely turn physical. The supremacy of one individual is established through dominance display, and the subordinate animal retreats. Serious conflicts over mating privileges or food resources occur mostly between animals of similar size. But even then the interactions between individuals are guided by behavioral mechanisms that avoid injury or death. It is of no advantage to the survival of a species if its members get killed during social contact. This doesn't mean that physical fights never occur, only that serious injury is the exception. Intense competition over mating rights may result in deep gashes and broken canine teeth or jaws. Many adult males sport big scars from wounds received in spring during the breeding season. But only rarely is the injury debilitating.

Females and cubs of the different species react dissimilarly to danger. Black bear females rarely defend their cubs. If threatened they send their offspring up into the safety of a tree and try to escape, luring pursuers away from their young. In the course of evolution, avoiding conflict has proven a more successful strategy than fighting. Brown bears and polar bears inhabit mostly open terrain that offers little to no escape from danger for the cubs. Thus, in both species, the mothers defend their offspring aggressively against any perceived threat, including other bears.

The difference between the species lies in the behavior of litter members during an altercation. Brown bear cubs either follow the confrontation as spectators on the sidelines a few yards away or they run off to hide. Polar bear cubs, on the other hand, as there is nowhere to conceal themselves on the open ice, stay with their mother. Right at her side is the safest place to be, and the charge looks even more daunting when mother and cubs rush forward in unison. Yet even in these scenarios physical contact is rare, although the threat display is most impressive. The object is to remove the threat without injury to the female. It's a balancing act. Before it escalates, the situation is usually defused through submissive gestures and displays of nonaggressiveness by the charged individual.

Occasionally, as habitats shrink and mankind increasingly regards nature as a wilderness playground, confrontations involve people. Polar bears are often considered the most dangerous and most aggressive of all bears. Being the most carnivorous species, they may well be. But attacks are still very rare, in part because of limited intersection between humans and *nanook'n*. People rarely wander onto the pack ice and along the floe edge (the limit of land-fast ice). But even those who explore the bear's icy realm are seldom approached aggressively. The animals focus on their natural prey and generally avoid humans. If they come closer, curiosity is usually the driving force. Only a starving animal might have an ulterior motive.

The most notorious species in regard to maulings is the grizzly. Some beliefs, regardless of how much they contradict reason, are engraved so deeply in our thinking that they have become a cultural heritage. So it has come about that the distorted image of an animal only vaguely resembling a bear haunts many a people. Its physical appearance is often the only aspect that does not conflict with reality. The rest is a wild synthesis of half-truths spiced strongly with imagination. Grizzlies traveling their remote high mountain retreats in the American and Canadian Rockies are considered guilty of indiscriminate manslaughter. A deep gulf separates reality and myth, its span getting wider the farther away you are from the present-day range of the animal.

The grizzly, its character vaguely based on the expedition reports of Lewis and Clark, became demonized as a popular villain of adventure literature in the nineteenth century. Since then the animal has never been able to entirely shake its reputation. The yellow press did its share to keep fear of bears alive and to add fuel to the flame. An uneventful encounter with no harm done to either party was not worth a single line. Thus the impression was given that the Grim Reaper circles in a holding pattern above every meeting of man and beast. Maulings and death do occur, no question about it. Between 1900 and 1980 a total of 19 people were killed by brown bears in national parks in North America. Between 1978 and 1994 two were killed in British Columbia. Several more people have died in maulings in Alaska since then. The number of nonfatal maulings is about 10 times higher.

While these figures may appear high at first glance, they are insignificant compared to deaths by other causes in national parks during the same period. Many more people drowned while swimming, boating or canoeing. The same holds true for fatalities caused by hypothermia or falls. But in those cases we regard the accidents as the result of stupidity, tragic misjudgment or simply bad luck. We consider ourselves to be in control, while in bear maulings it is the bear that calls the shots and acts. Victims until very recently were generally regarded as innocent bystanders drawn into the event without any wrongdoing. However, this is often not true. Grizzly attacks are almost invariably defense attacks – the animals regard themselves, their offspring or their food source as threatened.

In fights the combatants try to eliminate the opponent's most dangerous weapons, which in bears are their teeth. Consequently, the animals focus their attack on head or neck. Few males walk through life unscarred. Broken teeth, frayed ears and scars on muzzle and shoulders are evidence of the many battles fought.

In the vast majority of cases the bear was surprised or crowded by people. Frightened animals are left with two choices – flee or act on the principle that attack is the best possible mode of defense. As a rule, grizzlies show little interest in people and do not consider us two-legged beings as potential prey. If they are given the chance to avoid humans, in most instances they will take it. Thus the easiest remedy for avoiding trouble in bear country is to travel with eyes wide open and ears pricked, talking or singing loudly to announce one's presence near places with low visibility; to avoid prime feeding areas; and to give a bear his space when encountered. Most maulings involve lone hikers; there is no record of a grizzly attack on a group of more than three. There is safety in numbers, and if possible people should take advantage of that.

The behavioral repertoire of the bear is geared toward avoidance of injury, and this also applies to confrontations with man. Mostly it is our actions in an encounter that provide the final trigger and result in escalation of the situation. Bears are endowed by nature with physical strength, speed and agility far superior to a human's. We cannot successfully outrun or fight a bear. But if we adhere to the bear's code of ethics and conduct in a confrontation, we can lessen the likelihood of injury. Most charges are bluff charges. If we stand our ground, lift our arms to appear larger and talk firmly to the animal, the bear will most often retreat. Only if physical contact appears imminent should we drop to the ground, lie spread-eagled and cover our head and neck with our hands. Bears try to eliminate the most dangerous weapons of their opponents, and in other bears those are the jaws and teeth. In most cases a bear will run off after the threat has been eliminated.

Bear spray can be an effective deterrent in a grizzly encounter, but there are no brains in a can. The spray is effective only if directed into the grizzly's eyes. As this obviously requires the animal to be very close and invariably agitates the bear, it is a last-resort option. Bear spray cannot be used as a precaution like a mosquito repellent. The substance comes in aerosol cans and its active ingredient is capsicum, a natural chemical found in hot red peppers. After the irritant evaporates, the residual smell has been observed to actually attract bears.

On camping trips, supplies should never be stored in or near the tent, regardless of whether we consider them odorless or not. Our sense of smell hardly provides a competent criterion. Bears defend their food against fellow bruins and most certainly won't take kindly to our presence next to something to eat. And a fed bear usually becomes a dead bear. As the animals learn to associate humans with food, encounters become increasingly dangerous, until the bear has to be

The total population of brown bears in North America is estimated at 50,000 animals, 30,000 of which live in Alaska.

Their innate curiosity frequently brings juvenile bears into conflict with man, particularly if the animals learn to associate people with food or find nourishment around dwellings and on farms.

removed for public safety reasons. As relocations are expensive, and rarely successful, and in addition potentially negatively alter the naturally evolved population structure in the area the bears are relocated to, in most cases the animals are shot. Reconditioning is almost never successful.

We should not forget that we are but guests in the realm of the bear, and as such we should show respect for the animal. Ideally our presence should have no impact on the bears' behavior; the animals should be able to pursue their activities undisturbed. The best experiential and photographic opportunities arise when they are relaxed, totally ignoring us. If we act obtrusively, the animals only become nervous and wander off.

Black bears are often looked upon with contempt rather than respect. We consider them a nuisance but rarely a threat. Yet between 1979 and 1994 there were 71 cases of injury and nine deaths caused by black bears in British Columbia alone. These high figures are due in part to a much higher frequency of interaction – there are simply many more black bears than grizzlies. In addition, black bear habitats and human development overlap. Black bears are found in orchards, on farms and in our backyards. But black bears are also sometimes predatory on humans, something grizzlies almost never are. The predatory black bear is very rare, usually a desperate animal reverting to desperate measures.

Because it views humans as possible prey, the bear's attitude should dictate our behavior in a mauling. Should a black bear attack, the best line of defense is to fight back as hard as possible. Often the animal can be driven back. Pepper spray doesn't appear to work well for warding off black bears. They raid beehives and the nests of other communal insects without paying heed to the attacks of the angry occupants. As an evolutionary response to their source of food, the pain threshold around the black bear's eyes, nose and mouth seems to be too high for pepper spray to have much impact.

In bear country one's safety can never be taken for granted and is by no means guaranteed. However, the risk of being mauled by a bear is much smaller than the hazards of traffic that we take on almost every day, without expending as much as a thought on them.

· · ·

The old grizzly retreats from the spit after losing the moose carcass to the dominant male. Slowly, laboriously, he walks back toward the alder-covered hills. As he enters the brush he vanishes from view as if the land is welcoming his return. It will be a long, hard winter.

January

Chapter Twelve

On the Ice

Far north of the Arctic Circle, the land thirsts for light in the dead of winter as the desert thirsts for rain. At noon the world is immersed in a pale blue light. Heaven and earth fuse into one. On the southern horizon a faint glow bespeaks the position of the sun in more southerly realms. It is a promise of brighter and longer days to come.

Out on the ice, far from open water, *nanook* lies motionless next to a small pressure ridge, his eyes closed as if asleep. The slight twitching of his nose reveals that he is alert. The bear is hunting. Hidden beneath the snow, invisible from above, an *aglu* – the breathing hole of a seal – is located just a yard (1 m) ahead of him. *Nanook* has been lying in wait for over an hour. His sense of smell tells him that a seal has been using this hole recently. But his patience is starting to wear thin. Perhaps the seal heard his approach and abandoned this *aglu* in favour of another.

. . .

In winter, only about 20 percent of seal hunting consists of stalking the prey. But 80 percent of the time the bear is still hunting. The secret to success lies in knowing which *aglu* is in use. It also requires an ability to pinpoint the breathing hole without seeing it, as well as to correctly assess the snow conditions. If the snow is too hard or too deep, the bear can't break through the roof above the *aglu* in one pounce, and the seal escapes. Inuit hunters have copied this hunting technique, waiting motionless for hours on end for a seal to surface. The slightest movement carries through the ice as sound and the quarry will never appear. Just as Inuit hunters have to learn self-control and stoic endurance to master the "still hunt," so do bears. A young soul rarely possesses sufficient patience, and many a time the juvenile bear moves on to check other *aglus,* spooking his prey. The still hunt and the stalk are acquired techniques. The animals learn by watching their mother. Later, practice makes perfect. But even for a master hunter, more often than not the quarry escapes. Food and survival are never guaranteed.

When the ancestors of the polar bears began to live on the pack ice and along the floe edge, they were forced to adjust their diet. Marine mammals replaced roots and berries as the dominant food. The necessary behavioral adjustments for surviving on the ice were accompanied by anatomical adaptations. A lighter-colored animal stood out less against the ice. With better camouflage, hunting success was greater, which resulted in higher reproductive rates. The product of this selective process is today's almost pure white fur.

FACING PAGE: **Polar bears are superbly adapted to life on the ice. They are specialists in conserving energy and can wait motionless for hours at a seal breathing hole for their prey to surface.**

ABOVE: **In contrast to other bear species, fur covers the soles of their feet except for small pads. Their toes have short, curved claws that help them gain a firm foothold on the ice.**

155

In response to the cold environment the bears live in, their coat covers the entire body except for the footpads and the nose. The long, clear guard hair directs ultraviolet radiation toward the skin, which in contrast with grizzlies and black bears is black, to soak up the energy of the sun more efficiently. Their ears and tail are shorter than those of their ursine cousins in order to avoid heat loss. Their claws are short and strongly curved to provide a grip when climbing icy slopes and pressure ridges. Their feet are huge to distribute their weight on thin ice – a 1,100-pound (500 kg) polar bear can walk on ice that is too thin for a 220-pound (100 kg) human to walk on without snowshoes – and also to serve as paddles.

Nanook is as much at home in the water as on land. The bears' entire physique reflects the demands of a semiaquatic existence. They are built for swimming. Their body is teardrop-shaped to reduce drag in the water, and the long neck enables the animals to breathe more easily when swimming. Their fur is oily and doesn't retain water, which prevents ice from forming in their coat. Inuit hunters use pieces of polar bear fur dunked in a pot of water to apply a veneer of ice to the runners of their sleds. Afterward they dry the bear hide by simply shaking it. Polar bears roll in the snow after a swim to rid their coat of moisture.

The polar bear's swimming technique is different from a brown or black bear's. The latter dog-paddles with all four legs, whereas polar bears use only their arms to propel themselves. Their hind legs stretch out behind and serve as rudders. The animals can swim at a speed of 4.3 miles (7 km) per hour. They have been seen 60 miles (100 km) from the nearest land, still swimming strongly. Polar bears have also been observed swimming for 12 hours straight without showing signs of stress. They can dive as deep as 15 feet (4.5 m) and stay under water for over a minute. In the spring they frequently stalk seals hauled out on the ice by diving and then surfacing in the seal's escape hole. Inuit hunters tell of very large, obese males that hunt exclusively in the water to avoid walking. Apparently these massive animals have given up terrestrial pursuit of their quarry because of the physical restrictions imposed by their bulk.

· · ·

Suddenly the male opens his eyes. He rises without as much as a sound and freezes. His feet haven't moved, but his tendons and muscles tense until they are as taut as tightly coiled springs. Then he lunges forward. The roof of the *aglu* collapses under his weight and falls on top of the surprised seal. Before the animal is able to dive again, the bear grabs it by the head with his powerful jaws and yanks it out onto the ice in one swift motion. He drags his catch 50 feet (15 m) away from the hole, then bites the head of the seal several more times. Seal skulls are thin-boned, and the 100-pound (45 kg) animal is dead almost immediately. Without delay the bear starts feeding. He rips the carcass open and wolfs down chunks of blubber.

· · ·

Polar bears usually have one or two cubs per litter, and rarely three. In contrast to brown and black bears, which have six nipples – four on the chest and two on the abdomen – polar bear females have only four on the chest, which is regarded as an adaptation to the smaller average litter size.

A full-grown ringed seal has a food value of over 60,000 calories, two-thirds of which are contained in its fat. And it is the fat the bear focuses on. By grace of their physiological proficiency at recycling metabolic waste into amino acids, polar bears do not require proteins to rebuild muscle tissue. These building blocks remain within the body instead of being excreted. And there are benefits to focusing on fat. An active polar bear in the winter requires between 12,000 and 16,000 calories per day to maintain his weight. This translates into 4.4 pounds (2 kg) of blubber or 11 pounds (5 kg) of meat. As the stomach has a limited capacity, it makes sense for the bear to refrain from eating muscle tissue – for the same amount consumed, the net gain would be lower.

However, this logic seems inconclusive if the animal walks away from a partly eaten carcass. Often it is days between meals, and the stomach certainly digests quickly enough to warrant consuming the entire seal and not just parts thereof. But the energy content is just one factor to consider. There is a price to pay for feeding on meat. The digestion of protein produces nitrogen waste as a byproduct, which has to be removed from the system and excreted as urine. This requires water. Burning fat, on the other hand, produces – aside from energy – carbon dioxide, which can be exhaled, and water, which the body needs.

When we think of the Arctic as a habitat, inevitably we see temperature as the factor most hostile to life. Yet the cold is only indirectly a problem.

Thanks to their huge feet, even a thousand-pound polar bear is able to traverse ice too thin for a human to walk on. This female followed her eager cubs out onto the freshly frozen sea. When she started to break through, she spread her weight out by dragging her belly and legs.

The nose of a bear is a window to a world unknown to man. A polar bear can locate a seal lair by smell through 3 feet (1 m) of snow from half a mile away. Males sniff the footprints of females to determine their receptiveness during the mating period. When they encounter the tracks of a female in estrus, they follow them unerringly for many miles until they eventually catch up with her.

The limiting factor of life in the Far North is the availability of food and water. Although snow surrounds the animals with freshwater, it isn't readily available. Many mammals, including humans, cannot eat snow to obtain water. While snow will wet the palate, we actually become dehydrated if we try to consume it. In order to melt snow, our body has to provide energy, and the associated metabolic processes use up water. Humans end up with a negative balance in this calculation; bears, having vastly superior insulation, fare better. But the fundamental problem remains the same. A lot of energy has to be expended to melt the snow – it takes one calorie to heat a gram of water one degree Celsius. A bear can avoid this energy expenditure by eating fats.

Unlike bears, humans can't forsake drinking water by eating blubber, which would only reduce the amount we have to drink, not quench our thirst entirely. Anatomically we are simply not built for the Arctic. The human body is a product of an evolution that took place mostly in the tropics and subtropics. We compensate for our morphological shortcomings through technology.

Apart from excretion, humans lose water through sweating and breathing. The latter is a particular problem in a cold environment. Humidity decreases as temperatures drop. On cold days in temperate zones we complain of chapped and cracked lips. In the Arctic, dehydration is much more pronounced. A person traveling at –22°F (–30°C) on the Barren Lands has to drink about a gallon (3.8 l) of water a day to compensate for water lost through breathing.

The polar bear, on the other hand, evolved in this forbidding realm. The animals have enlarged nasal cavities that endow the bears with their straight Roman nose, in contrast to the dish-shaped face of their closest relative, the grizzly. Intricately arranged turbinate bones fill the nasal passage like a sponge and are covered with a mucous membrane. The function of the nasal passage is primarily particle removal and the warming up and humidifying of inhaled air. Since it works like an exchange system, it also dehumidifies and cools the air to be exhaled. The system works so efficiently that even on the coldest days no vapor cloud is detectable in front of a polar bear's face when the animal is breathing through its nose. The water budget may even influence the animal's hunting style during the coldest months of the year. The still hunt, because it's less physically demanding, allows the animal to breathe through its nose.

. . .

For 30 minutes the large male feeds on his kill. Then he gets up, moves a few yards away and rolls in the snow to clean his coat of blood. He also licks his paws and front legs. Washing is an integral part of the meal for every polar bear, as future hunting success depends on cleanliness. A stained coat is more visible on the ice. In addition, the bear's prey may be warned off by the smell of blood. Finally abandoning the carcass, the male walks off, leaving the meat and viscera behind.

. . .

Ringed seals are the main food source of polar bears. To maintain his weight a male has to catch one about every five days. Preying on other animals allows the bears to space their hunts further apart. These other animals include the largest true seal in the Arctic, the bearded seal, which weighs as much as 770 pounds (350 kg). Polar bears sometimes also attack walrus, a formidable and very dangerous quarry even for a full-grown male. Occasionally they are able to catch beluga whales when they get trapped by the ice or the outgoing tide. The animals also scavenge on carcasses of bowhead whales. Attracted by the smell, dozens of bears will congregate and share the food bonanza for weeks.

Nanook has no natural enemies in his Arctic home, except perhaps the orca, or killer whale, according to unsubstantiated reports. The polar bear is the supreme predator of the Far North. But a threat to his continued existence may come from an unexpected direction. The health of a bear is directly affected by what he eats. All bears have intestinal parasites. Nematodes and fish tapeworms flourish in coastal brown bears, which pick up the parasites from salmon. Seals are carriers of the Trichinella worm. As a result, almost every polar bear is infected with this tiny parasite, which in humans causes the disease trichinosis. Some polar expeditions faltered when people consumed polar bear meat without cooking it properly. In contrast to humans, otherwise healthy bears appear to have few problems coexisting with the parasite.

Bears have always had to cope with natural diseases. What has changed is that their food source now carries not only parasites but also man-made chemicals. High concentrations of pesticides, heavy metals and PCBs (polychlorinated biphenyls) have been discovered in polar bears. These pollutants are funneled through the food chain. The great unknown is the impact that these substances will have on the reproductive success and survival rate of the bears. As it is, global warming is shortening their hunting season along the southern extent of their distribution, and the effect is measurable. In Hudson Bay the average weight of the animals and average litter size in the years following cold winters is greater than after mild winters. Will the bears be able to cope with any additional stress? Polar bears, unbeknownst to them, have helped direct our attention to the fact that local actions have global implications. This realization has resulted in international cooperation on environmental issues – the bear has inspired us to clean up our act.

. . .

The male walks into an uncertain future as he vanishes into the blue light of the Arctic day. But as long as there is sea ice for a large part of the year and as long as there are seals, there will be *nanook* – if we let him be.

Epilogue

The Future of Bears

Overnight the frosty breath of the north wind has decorated the tall yellow grass with delicate snow crystals. The waves of the lake heave in languid motion, their vigor subdued by new grease ice along the shore. It is late October, and winter sends its regards from the northwest. On the Alaska Peninsula the sun is no longer able to warm the land on its low traverse across the sky. Last night the temperature dropped to 5°F (–15°C), and it hasn't warmed up much since.

Protected from the piercing cold by a heavy jacket, mitts and fleece hat, I sit alone on a sandy spit at the mouth of the Brooks River in Katmai National Park. The birch trees along the bank point with naked fingers. The river is still flowing – the current prevents ice from choking its course. In the clear water I notice the dark red body of a single sockeye salmon moving slowly upstream. Apart from some late arrivals swimming in total disregard of the masses, the sockeye salmon migration has come to an end. Only days ago hundreds of fish lay scattered across the riverbed. Dozens of salmon carcasses floated in eddies and were washed up on the beach. Now the shore is swept clean of any fish remains, and the eddies swirl free of flotsam.

The conclusion of this year's fishing season was matched by a sudden exodus of bears. Four days ago I counted 20 different grizzlies as they meandered along the river or drifted with the flow searching for food. Yesterday I saw four – a single male and a female with two yearling cubs. Today, in the two hours I have spent sitting quietly at the water's edge, I haven't detected a single bear. Their food source gone, the animals are leaving the river to search for berries on the mountain slopes and prepare for hibernation.

The murmur of the water sends my thoughts traveling. I am fantasizing about a warmer climate and a hot cup of tea when I am suddenly called back to the here and now by the sound of breaking branches. Sixty yards (55 m) upstream the grizzly family appears at the river's edge. The cubs trail a few feet behind their mother, their coats shiny and thick. Roly-poly in stature, they have obviously had a good summer and fall. As the female reaches the water, she glances back to check on her cubs, then scans the areas on both sides of the river. For a second her eyes rest on me, then she bends down and starts to drink, undisturbed by my presence.

The Brooks River, like other bear-viewing places such as McNeil or Pack Creek, Anan Creek and the Khutzeymateen, have shown that bears and people can share the land peacefully. If a bear doesn't feel threatened, the animal will mostly ignore a human visitor to its domain. Bears watch, learn and remember. My behavior over the past few

160

weeks has enabled the female to predict what I will do. Bears have to survive in their world, and avoiding something that poses no threat is a waste of energy. And as she hasn't learned to associate a food reward with humans, she ignores these strange two-legged creatures.

When the bear appears I abandon my spot on the spit and walk back toward the trees. Although I have never been approached aggressively by a grizzly in over 20 years of working in bear country, I like to keep my options open. The narrow sand-bank leaves me with no route of retreat should it become necessary to avoid the bear family. Beneath a small pine at the edge of the forest, I sit down on a fallen log. The cubs, being young and curious, follow my every movement with their eyes. Their mother, secure in herself, pays me no heed after the initial perfunctory acknowledgment. Noisily she slurps up the cold water. Her thirst finally quenched, she looks up, gives her surroundings another superficial inspection, and then slowly follows the river downstream.

Her stride is heavy, almost as if she is contemplating every step before she puts down her foot. When she reaches the spot where I was sitting just moments before, she sniffs the ground. Her cubs display more interest in the new smell. They paw the sand and then roll in the little depression I left behind. Meanwhile their mother has continued her stroll along the water's edge. Every step she makes brings her a step closer to me. She passes within 25 yards (23 m). Her cubs finally abandon their infatuation with my odor and race after her. When they draw level with me they lift their heads. Nose held high, both make a few steps in my direction. Curiosity overcomes apprehension as they walk closer, then nervousness over their own boldness wins out and they quickly run after their mother.

My heart pounds in my chest. In my hand I hold a marine flare pointed forward, the pull string wrapped around my finger. The female is clearly more comfortable in my presence than I am in hers – she never even turned her head. I find it hard to fully reciprocate the trust she puts in me. If anything, she should be the more nervous one. Yet it is in me, not in her, that some hidden primeval fear still lurks. She had my number weeks ago – I get as much attention as a boulder on the side of the trail.

I am always stunned by the tolerance these animals show toward people if given half a chance. They are amazingly forgiving of our unintentional and even deliberate transgressions. If every mistake we make and every stupid act was punished, maulings would be an everyday occurrence. Instead, if they happen they make headlines because they are so rare. After years of watching people around grizzlies, the most striking impression I am left with is the lenience these animals display toward humans, even when faced with some of the most deplorable, inconsiderate and aggressive behavior imaginable. Fear is a terrible counselor, but misplaced confidence and contempt are none the better.

Bears are only bears, not teddies, but not monsters either. They are but impressive denizens of the pristine wilderness that demand our respect. Dread can change into appreciation only if understanding replaces ignorance. The future of the great bears depends on education, which makes places such as Brooks Camp invaluable. Few

return home without a changed perspective on bears. Our apprehension about the great beasts is simply fear of the unknown.

The bear family continues along the shore of Naknek Lake. When the female and her cubs are about 200 yards (180 m) ahead of me, I slowly follow, heading back to camp. My steps fall into the tracks left by the huge animal. She and her cubs are the last bears to leave the river. They will be back next year, and the year after. Her cubs will use this stream when they are on their own and so will their cubs, as long as fish spawn in these waters.

There is a future for the bears of North America if we provide them with space to live their lives. They are amazingly resourceful, adaptable and indulgent animals. As soon as we realize that life is indivisible, as soon as we understand that what befalls nature will invariably at some point befall us, we may be more willing to show bears a small measure of the tolerance they display toward us. That is all that is required to coexist. It will be to our benefit to live in the presence of these monarchs of the northern wilderness, to share the land with them, to allow them to provide us with inspiration and teach us humility. There is value in untouched places and wild animals. I hope the message continues to spread, even back to the driver who was generous enough to give me a lift all those years ago. Considering the growing change in the general public's attitude toward wildlife – and bears in particular – the future looks promising.

Appendix

Bears of the World

What makes a bear a bear? Being both generalists and opportunists, bears defy generalization. They are highly intelligent, learn quickly and easily adapt to new and changing environmental conditions. While this combination of traits embodies the essence of bears, it lacks in particulars, and anyone making absolute statements about bears is invariably – sooner or later – proven wrong. However, a purely academic approach does allow us to categorize these animals.

The family Ursidae, the bears, consists of eight species, six of which – the brown bear, polar bear, American black bear, Asiatic black bear, sun bear and sloth bear – are closely related; they comprise the subfamily Ursinae, the true bears. The spectacled bear and the giant panda each have their own family, respectively the Tremarctinae, or short-faced bears, and the Ailuropodinae. From a systematic perspective, bears belong in the order Carnivora, the meat eaters, a diverse group of animals totaling 254 species. All carnivores have a common ancestry: they evolved from the miacids, a group of mammals that lived 60 to 70 million years ago.

Most early carnivores diverged quickly from a more herbivorous diet to eating meat. Bears, on the other hand, evolved to use more generalized sources of food. The ability to switch between a herbivorous and a carnivorous diet, depending on availability, is unique to the bears. All living bear species are opportunistic feeders, although some more so than others. Even the highly specialized panda will occasionally add some carrion to its diet of bamboo. Neither does the sloth bear eat only insects nor the polar bear rely exclusively on marine mammals for food.

Physically, bears are large, compact carnivores. To support their weight they walk on the soles of their feet, a gait called plantigrade. They have powerful legs, and their feet carry long, non-retractable claws. All bears have a short tail. Their eyes and outer ears are small, and the sense of smell is well developed. The animals' teeth display adaptations for an omnivorous diet: the carnassials are reduced and the molars are enlarged and wide-crowned. To reflect the increased demand that vegetable matter imposes on the digestive system, their intestines are longer than in typical carnivores, measuring in most bears between six and ten times their body length.

The ancestral home of bears is the temperate zone of the northern hemisphere, which is characterized by seasonally abundant food sources but also by periods of acute shortage. Bears adapted to intervals in which little nourishment was available by moving into a state of suspended animation and living off their fat resources. Numerous mammal species such as marmots and ground squirrels follow a similar pattern, but all of them are substantially smaller than bears. As the length of gestation is proportional to the body size of the parent, pregnancy in bears lasts too long to take place entirely during their active phase. Consequently the animals were forced to adapt, using a strategy that enabled them to hibernate during pregnancy. In a prolonged fasting period the energy to maintain necessary bodily functions is provided by burning fat. However, the placenta through which the fetus is nourished is unable to transport the large molecules of fatty acids through its membrane. The energy required by the fetus is therefore supplied by amino acids, the building blocks of muscle tissue. To avoid severe depletion of muscle mass in the mother, the cubs are born in a premature state and then raised on milk rich in fat, which after birth can be absorbed through the gastrointestinal tract. As a result, bears give birth to tiny cubs that weigh between 1/300 and 1/600 of the body weight of the mother. Although bears in tropical regions don't hibernate, they still follow this reproductive method inherited from their ancestors.

Bears are thought to be induced ovulators, meaning that a physical stimulus is required for the ovaries to release an ovum. All animals for which induced ovulation has been confirmed have a penis bone called a baculum; in a grizzly it is about the size of a ballpoint pen. After copulation and fertilization, the initial zygote develops until it reaches the blastocyst stage, which takes 10 to 14 days. Implantation of the blastocyst in the wall of the uterus is delayed until the female enters hibernation or a similar quiescent stage, which can be several months later and is likely hormonally induced.

THE BLACK BEAR

The most common bear in North America, with a total population of around 450,000, is also the smallest. An adult individual stands 35 to 40 inches (89–102 cm) tall at the shoulder when on all fours and measures from 4.5 to 6 feet (137–182 cm) in length. Its average weight is 125 to 600 pounds (57–272 kg), and the heaviest recorded individual registered over 900 pounds (400 kg) on the scale. The fur color ranges from black and dark brown to creamy white. Sexual maturity is reached at three to four years for females, and a year later for males. Lifespan in the wild is mostly 20 to 25 years, with some individuals reaching 30 years or, in rare cases, even a few years older.

THE POLAR BEAR

The total worldwide polar bear population is about 50,000. Adult animals stand 6 to 11 feet (180–335 cm) tall. They can weigh 440 to 1,320 pounds (200–600 kg), with some males exceeding 1,800 pounds (815 kg). The fur's underwool is creamy white and the guard hairs are long and clear. Their skin is black to better absorb heat. Females reach sexual maturity at four to seven years, males at six or seven years. Life expectancy for males is the late teens and for females the early to mid-twenties, with some individuals reaching their late twenties.

THE BROWN BEAR

The total population of brown bears in North America is about 50,000, and worldwide 125,000 to 150,000. Their size ranges from 5.5 to 7.5 feet (180–250 cm), with coastal brown bears reaching 10 feet in length. Weights range generally from 210 to 900 pounds (95–408 kg). Along coastal Alaska and on Kamchatka large males may exceed 1,500 pounds (680 kg). Fur color ranges from blond to a very dark brown. The guard hairs of interior bears are frequently tipped with white, giving the animal a grizzled appearance. Females reach sexual maturity at five years, males at six to seven. Life expectancy for males is 20 to 25 years, with females often reaching their late twenties.

THE SUN BEAR

The sun bear (*Helarctos malayanus*) is the smallest of all bears, with adults measuring four to five feet (120–150 cm) in length. Their weight ranges from 60 to 145 pounds (27–65 kg), with males 10 to 20 percent larger than females. Their fur is glossy black and less than half an inch (1.25 cm) long. A crescent-shaped golden or whitish patch marks the chest. The feet have bare soles and long claws, which is seen as an adaptation for climbing trees. Sun bears have a long tongue, which is thought to be used to gather honey and insects from tree cavities. They have proportionally large heads compared to other bears.

Sun bears live in lowland rain forest in Southeast Asia as far west as Bangladesh. The eastern extent of their range lies in Vietnam; the southern limit is Sumatra and Borneo. They are omnivores, feeding on termites, small vertebrates, palm shoots, rain-forest fruits and wild bee nests. They are much affected by large-scale habitat destruction through logging and also by poaching.

Very little is known of sun bears' behavior in the wild. In zoos animals have lived to 25 years. Cubs appear to be born throughout the year, with litters usually of one or two. At birth sun bears weigh about 10 ounces (325 g).

In relation to their body size, sun bears have – along with polar bears – the largest canines. As their diet does not suggest the need for such long teeth, it is assumed that they play a role in social behavior, particularly during the mating season.

THE SLOTH BEAR

Sloth bears (*Melursus ursinus*) have a disheveled appearance. Their coat is long and shaggy, particularly on the shoulders, and usually dusty black in color, though cinnamon and reddish individuals have been reported. The animals have a cream-colored U- or Y-shaped chest patch and the muzzle is pale and short-haired. Sloth bears can close their nostrils at will, protecting the animal from insects when raiding beehives or termite mounds.

Sloth bears live in grasslands and lowland woodlands in India, Sri Lanka and southern Nepal. They have also been reported in Bhutan and Bangladesh. These bears grow to five to six feet (150–180 cm) in length and reach a maximum weight of 310 pounds (140 kg). Females are 30 percent smaller than males. In zoos sloth bears have lived up to 40 years.

The animals mate from May to July. The females give birth to one or two cubs, though rarely three. They are born in an underground den, where they remain for the first several months. Mothers are known to carry their young on their backs for extended times.

Sloth bears feed extensively on termites and have special adaptations for consuming their tiny prey efficiently. The innermost upper incisors are missing, creating a gap. In addition, their naked lips can be protruded. In combination, these physical traits enable the sloth bear to suck up the termites; the noise they make when feeding can be heard from 100 yards (90 m) away.

THE SPECTACLED OR ANDEAN BEAR

The spectacled bear (*Tremarctos ornatus*) is the only living representative of the Tremarctinae, the short-faced bears, which until the end of the last ice age were widespread in the Americas and represented by at least 25 species. The spectacled bear is South America's only bear; it lives in the Andes and outlying mountain ranges from western Venezuela south to Bolivia.

The animals grow up to five to six feet long (150–180 cm) and stand two to three feet (60–90cm) at the shoulder. Males reach 340 pounds (155 kg) in weight. Females rarely grow heavier than 180 pounds (82 kg). Cubs weigh 10 to 11.5 ounces (300–360 g) at birth. Spectacled bears have distinctive whitish or cream markings around their eyes that usually extend down the throat and chest. Their thick coat is black, brown or, rarely, reddish in color.

These animals are found in a wide range of habitats from rain forest to coastal scrub desert. Possibly because of persecution by man and loss of habitat, they are found most commonly in dense forest. Although some individuals inhabit both higher and much lower elevations, spectacled bears appear to favor moist forest between 6,000 and 8,800 feet (1,800–2,700 m) above sea level. The bears have not been documented in areas devoid of bromeliads and fruits, their favored foods. However, they will also eat berries, grasses, orchid bulbs, cactus flowers, insects and small vertebrates such as mice, rabbits and birds. The animals construct nest platforms in trees to feed from and to sleep in.

Female spectacled bears reach sexual maturity between four and seven years of age. The mating season extends from April to June. Cubs – usually one or two, rarely three – are born from November to February.

THE GIANT PANDA

The giant panda (*Ailuropoda melanoleuca*), with its black ears, eye patches, muzzle, legs and shoulders contrasting with its otherwise white coat, is one of the most recognizable animals in the world. It is also one of the rarest. By recent estimates (2004) about 1,500 animals still live in the wilds of remote mountain ranges in central and western China, mainly in Sichuan, Shaanxi and Gansu provinces. The animals inhabit mountain forests with a dense bamboo understory at elevations between 4,000 and 11,000 feet (1,200–3,350 m).

Their diet consists almost exclusively (99 percent) of the branches, stems and leaves of over 30 bamboo species. To crush the tough shoots the animals have wide molars and strong jaw muscles. Depending on the parts of the bamboo the animals are feeding on, an adult giant panda can consume between 25 and 80 pounds (11–36 kg) of food per day.

Full-grown giant pandas range in body length from 64 to 76 inches (160–190 cm). Males reach 275 pounds (125 kg) in weight. Females are 10 to 20 percent lighter, obtaining a maximum weight of 220 pounds (100 kg).

Giant pandas have the smallest newborns relative to the size of the mother of all the higher mammals. The cubs weigh four to six ounces (113–170 g) at birth – lighter than an apple. Although females frequently give birth to two young, only one usually survives. Giant panda cubs may stay with their mother for up to two years. Their life expectancy in the wild is unknown, but in zoos they have reached an age of 35 years.

The front paw of the giant panda has six digits. The radial sesamoid (the wrist bone) is extended, forming an opposable thumb for holding bamboo. In contrast to other bears, the male genitalia point backward, as in the red panda.

THE ASIATIC BLACK BEAR

The Asiatic black bear (*Ursus thibetanus*) is the closest relative to the American black bear, and looks much like it. However, it has round, more pronounced ears and a distinct white V-shaped patch on its chest that gives the animal its Asian common name, the moon bear.

Asiatic black bears have a wide but now disjunct range in southern Asia. They occur in the mountains of Afghanistan, Pakistan, northern India and Nepal and east to Vietnam and southern China. They are also found in northeastern China, southeastern Russia, on Taiwan and in Japan, on the islands of Honshu and Shikoku. Because of persecution by humans, mostly for medicinal purposes, they are today a threatened species.

Adult individuals grow to four to six feet in length (120–180 cm). Males range in weight from 220 to 440 pounds (100–200kg). Adult females are substantially smaller, reaching 110 to 275 pounds (50–125 kg).

Asiatic black bears live in temperate mountain forests. They occur at altitudes as high as 9,900 feet (3,000 m) but they also frequent the lowlands, particularly in winter. Depending on the season, the animals use different food sources, primarily plants. During the fall mast their diet is dominated by nuts, acorns and berries. They will feed on carrion if available and occasionally attack livestock.

The breeding season of the Asiatic black bear varies regionally. In northern parts of their range, mating usually takes place in early summer. In Pakistan, however, the animals breed in October. The cubs are born in the winter den and the young usually remain with their mother for two to three years. Females have sometimes been reported with cubs of different ages.

Further Reading

Alaska Geographic Society. "Alaska's Bears." *Alaska Geographic* 20:4.

Brown, Gary. *The Great Bear Almanac*. New York: Lyons & Burford, 1993.

Craighead, Frank C. *Track of the Grizzly*. San Francisco: Sierra Club Books, 1979.

Craighead, Lance. *Bears of the World*. Stillwater, MN: Voyageur Press, 2000.

DeBruyn, Terry. *Walking with Bears: One Man's Relationship with Three Generations of Wild Bears*. New York: Lyons Press, 1999.

Domico, Terry, and Mark Newman. *Bears of the World*. New York: Facts on File, 1988.

Furtman, Michael. *Black Bear Country*. Minnetonka, MN: NorthWord Press, 1998.

Herrero, Steven. *Bear Attacks: Their Causes and Avoidance*. New York: Lyons & Burford, 1985.

Lynch, Wayne. *Bears: Monarchs of the Northern Wilderness*. Seattle: The Mountaineers, 1993.

Mangelsen, Thomas. *Polar Dance: Born of the North Wind*. Omaha, NE: Images of Nature, 1997.

McMillion, Scott. *Mark of the Grizzly: True Stories of Recent Bear Attacks and the Hard Lessons Learned*. Helena, MT: Falcon, 1998.

Murie, Adolph. *The Grizzlies of Mt. McKinley*. Seattle: University of Washington Press, 1987.

Ovsyanikov, Nikita. *Polar Bear: Living with the White Bear*. Stillwater, MN: Voyageur Press, 1996.

Powell, R.A., J.W. Zimmerman and D.E. Seaman. *Ecology and Behavior of North American Black Bears: Home Ranges, Habitat and Social Organization*. New York: Chapman & Hall, 1997.

Rockwell, David. *Giving Voice to Bear: North American Indian Rituals, Myths, and Images of the Bear*. Niwot, CO: Roberts Rinehart, 1991.

Russell, Charles. *Spirit Bear: Encounters with the White Bear of the Northern Rainforest*. Toronto: Key Porter Books, 1994.

Russell, Charles, and Maureen Enns. *Grizzly Seasons: Life with the Brown Bears of Kamchatka*. Toronto: Random House, 2003.

Schneider, Bill. *Where the Grizzly Walks: The Future of the Great Bear*. Helena, MT: Falcon, 2004.

Schullery, Paul. *Lewis and Clark among the Grizzlies: Legend and Legacy in the American West*. Helena, MT: Falcon, 2002.

Smith, David. *Backcountry Bear Basics*. Seattle: The Mountaineers, 1997.

Stirling, Ian. *Bears: Majestic Creatures of the Wild*. Emmaus, PA: Rodale Press, 1993.

———. *Polar Bears*. Markham, ON: Fitzhenry & Whiteside, 1998.

Turbak, Gary. *Grizzly Bears*. Vancouver, BC: Raincoast Books, 1997.

Van Daele, Larry. *The History of Bears on the Kodiak Archipelago*. Anchorage, AK: Alaska Natural History Association, 2003.

Van Tighem, Kevin. *Bears: An Altitude SuperGuide*. Canmore, AB: Altitude Publishing, 1997.

Wakeman, Dan, and Wendy Shymanski. *Fortress of Bears: The Khutzeymateen Grizzly Bear Sanctuary*. Surrey, BC: Heritage House, 2003.

Walker, Tom, and Larry Aumiller. *River of Bears*. Stillwater, MN: Voyageur Press, 1993.

Zhi, Lü, and George Schaller. *Giant Pandas in the Wild: Saving an Endangered Species*. Denville, NJ: Aperture, 2002.

Websites

Bear Trust International: www.beartrust.org

Brown Bear Resources: www.brownbear.org

Great Bear Foundation: www.greatbear.org

Interagency Grizzly Bear Committee: www.fs.fed.us/r1/wildlife/igbc

International Association for Bear Research and Management (IBA): www.bearbiology.com

IUCN Polar Bear Specialist Group: pbsg.npolar.no

North Cascades Grizzly Bear Outreach Project (GBOP): www.bearinfo.org

Index

Photo Credits

All photographs by Matthias Breiter except: **20-21** Michael Mauro/Minden Pictures;
35 Jim Brandenburg/Minden Pictures; **71** Rinie Van Muers/Foto Natura/Minden Pictures;
110 Sumio Harada/Minden Pictures; **113** Nick Jans/nickjans.com; **167** Art Wolfe/firstlight.ca;
168 E.A. Kuttapan/Nature Picture Library; **169** Gerry Ellis/Minden Pictures;
170 Sichuan/Daniel A. Edell/Maxximages.com; **171** Juergen and Christine Sohns/Maxximages.com